AD   RES
IN CHRIST

EXPANDED EDITION 3

BY
ANDRE RABE

ISBN: 978-0-9563346-2-6

Published by Andre Rabe Publishing.

Contents

FOREWORD

Andre's writing celebrates the fact that liberty is fully restored to humanity! What a joy to read insight, to grasp or rather be grasped by that which has been from the beginning. This book will revolutionise the thinking of many. It carries the unction of the Spirit of Christ to proclaim good news to the poor, to heal the broken heart, to set the captive free and to open the eyes of the blind.

Multitudes of believers have become neutralised in clumsy organisations that tax their time, finance and energy instead of revealing the risen Christ in them. This truth alone will mobilise believers to arise in the full realisation of His glory in the flesh. Nations with their leaders will be irrsistibly attracted to the brightness of your rising! I anticipate a global explosion of ordinary lives living in the full impact and implication of their true identity and eternal destiny realised.

Great change is coming to church-life as we know it. Many believers find a fresh expression in a smaller home environment rather than the impersonal big building context (Often spelt, contest!). What needs reformation though, is not in the first place the size or structure of church expression but the content of its message! Unless the fundamental ingredient of our understanding of the finished work of Christ is grasped by engraved spirit revelation, the smaller compact package of the home-church will soon become the same baggage that neutralised and paralysed believers for ages. "A little leaven leavens the whole lump' says Paul in Gal.5:6-10. He clearly refers to religious tradition, in this case, circumcision that represents personal contribution and performance in order to distinguish and qualify the individual. Even the slightest emphasis on personal effort and contribution, nullifies the faith that grace reveals and makes gratitude phoney. Any presence in our belief, even insignificantly small, of something we still have to do in order to obtain favour from God, nullifies the power of the cross and puts us back under the law of performance. *"While we compete and compare with one another we are without understanding!"* 2 Cor. 10:12.

Francois Du Toit.

Hermanus, South Africa.

The Genetic Code of God

In Christ, God preserved the live-code, the original thought and design of man. He never had a plan B for a lesser man or an inferior relationship.

Life Awakened

It does not move; it does not grow; it does not breath - yet it is alive. It certainly looks dead, this small object I hold within my hand, but deep within it is hidden a mysterious life. Yes, it might seem small and lifeless now, but once awakened it has the potential to produce an abundance of life out of all proportion to its current state.

A seed does not move, breath, grow or do anything else that we associate with being alive. Yet within this seemingly lifeless container lies one of the greatest wonders of life - the genetic code, the logic, that is capable of unleashing a burst of life. There might be a forest in that single seed. As someone once said: "You can count the seeds in an apple, but can you count the apples in a seed?" All it needs is to be awakened.

Different seeds have different types of dormancy and different triggers that break this dormancy. In some seeds, germination is triggered by moisture, in others by light, yet in others by a combination of stimuli. I once read an amazing story about seed that was discovered in an ancient Egyptian tomb. Grain was deposited into a Pharaoh's tomb together with his remains. Thousands of years later men discovered that grain. When they planted some of those seeds, they germinated. The death concealed within the tomb could not overcome the life preserved within those seeds!

Man originated in God. Although dormant, the seed of God, His genetic code, remains within man. Peter wrote about the fact that we were born not of corruptible seed, but incorruptible - the word of God that lives and abides forever. (1Pet 1:23) Incorruptible seed - think about that. This seed might have been separated from the tree of its origin, it might have been trampled under foot ... but it is incorruptible! The logic of its origin remains in tact. There is an environment that can cause this seed to germinate. There are words that contain the spirit environment that causes this spirit seed within man to germinate and produce resurrection life. A person might have no interest in God, and could have been in this state of spiritual death for many years. Oh, but when words of life enter, the very death or tomb in which he lives, becomes a womb; a womb that incubates the very life of God.

Often people speak about 'children of the Devil' and 'children of God' as if God and the Devil are on the same level as creators. Ridiculous! There is only one Creator, one God and one Father of us all (Eph 4:6). And in the previous chapter Paul writes: "*I bow my knees before the Father of our Lord Jesus Christ, from Whom every family in heaven and on earth is named.*" The only thing Satan ever gave birth to is lies. Throughout the centuries man has adopted this foreign 'father' by submitting to his way of thinking, thereby adopting a foreign identity. Yet submitting to this lie did not change the truth of mankind's origin, nor did it make the devil an actual creator or father. It is in this context that Jesus said: 'You are of your father the devil' referring to their way of thinking and consequent actions, immediately qualifying it in the next sentence by saying: 'he is the father of lies'.

I love the way in which the Message translates John 1:12:

But whoever did want him,
who believed he was who he claimed
and would do what he said,
He made to be their true selves,
their child-of-God selves.

For even if there are so-called gods whether in heaven or on earth, ... yet for us there is but one God, the Father, from whom are all things and we exist for Him; and one Lord, Jesus Christ, by whom are all things, and we exist through Him. (1 Cor 8:5,6)

For surely You are our Father, even though Abraham does not know us and Israel does not acknowledge us; You, O Lord, are still our Father... (Is 63:16)

In Christ, God preserved the life-code, the original thought and design of man. He never had a plan B for a lesser man or an inferior relationship. Christ remained the reference and measure of man. "*that [we might arrive] at really mature manhood (the completeness of personality which is nothing less than the standard height of Christ's own perfection), the measure of the stature of the fullness of the Christ and the completeness found in Him.*" (Eph 4:13 AMP.) When the Logos became flesh, the word that was in the beginning - plan A - was once again displayed in all its fullness and the great awakening began. The ignorance induced dormancy was broken. The fullness of Gods purpose was made visible.

An Unexpected Journey

At the age of 16 I lived in a town called Ermelo in South Africa. My older brother, Francois Rabe, had left home a number of years earlier, so seeing him over weekends was a real treat. One day, he phoned to tell me that he would be taking me to visit an exciting youth group over the weekend. This group was based in the rugged beauty of the White River area.

He fetched me on the Friday and we drove about 3 hours to our destination. At the top of a hill, we finally stopped at a hotel called Petra. A few hundred young people from all over the country, as well as many other parts of the world, were gathered there.

A man named Francois Du Toit spoke during the weekend. To this day I have no idea what he said, but I do know that something within me shouted 'YES'. My spirit endorsed what was said, although my mind did not yet understand it. There was a burst of energy within me and a new found awareness of God's closeness, yet I could not articulate it. The weekend came to an end. I could not tell you anything I learned, yet I knew I could never be the same again. My spirit had grasped an insight so great that it would take months to transfer that knowledge to my mind! Spirit words broke the dormancy within me and began the activation of a new life.

Through the years I've learned that my spirit is able to grasp truths long before my mind is capable of understanding them logically. Jesus said that His words are spirit and life - John 6:63. These words do not appeal to the logic of man. They aim deeper, to the spirit of man. The aim of this writing is not your head, but your spirit. My appeal is not to your intellect alone, but to something much deeper. This is why, after reading Jesus' words for years, we find them fresh and life-giving. They contain more than natural logic; they contain spirit and the amount of revelation contained in them, cannot be measured. To receive the spirit of what is said, we need to engage more than our minds. You have within you the ability to hear and understand spirit truths that completely bypass your natural mind. We need the Spirit of God to connect with our spirits to reveal to us spiritual truths.

Paul expressed this same truth in the following way: "*which things also we speak, not in words taught by human wisdom, but in words taught by the Holy Spirit, interpreting spiritual things by spiritual words or, combining spiritual ideas with spiritual words..*" 1 Cor 2:13

I want to invite you, right now, to raise your expectation

of what you want out of this book. It was not written to merely inform you, so expect more than information. It was not written to simply adjust your thinking, so expect more than adjusted thoughts. Intimate encounter with God is the greatest source of inspiration. Expect encounter with God. He desires nothing less. Allow your spirit to soak in the heart of what is said and respond to the Father's love. Allow the spirit contained within these words to bring about a fusion between you and God. Faith is the catalyst that brings about this fusion.

The Nature of Revelation

Revelation implies seeing and realising things we did not know before. One of the greatest obstacles to revelation, is only allowing thoughts that confirm what we already know. We find security and comfort in what we already know and, therefore, any insight that challenges our current knowledge can easily be rejected, simply because it's new. I want to take this a step further and say that revelation often implies acknowledging that what we have believed up to now ... is wrong!

Once again this is a transformation that reaches far beyond our intellect alone. This has to do with the receptiveness of our hearts. Our thinking is often influenced and conformed by our peers, much more than what we are willing to admit. What we think others think of us, influences our thinking! Jesus said of some *"for they loved the praise of men more than the praise of*

God." John 12:43. Once we become more desperate for intimacy with Christ than for the approval of man, we are positioned to receive from Him, insights far above what we could ever imagine.

Fear of the unknown, fear of losing the approval of others, fear is what closes our receptiveness to the workings of God within us. But love is a force that overcomes fear. In His presence there is an atmosphere of love and trust that enables us to let go of all the uncertainties and hesitations, and simply let Him say whatever He wants to say. Some might be so conditioned to rely on others to confirm that what they heard was right, or wrong, that they have no confidence in their own ability to hear. Let me state it loud and clear: Our confidence is firstly not in our ability to hear, but in God's ability to accurately communicate and reveal Himself! And he needs no interpreter! He made you; He knows how to speak to you.

Hear what our Father believes concerning you:

Philippians 2:13 *"for it is God who works in you both to will and to do according to his good pleasure."*

Trust His workings within you!

Romans 15:14 *"And I myself also am persuaded of you, my brothers, that you also are full of goodness, filled with all knowledge, able also to admonish one another."*

Come to the same persuasion!

1John 2:20,21 *"But you have an anointing from the Holy One,*

14

and you know all things. I have not written to you because you do not know the truth, but because you know it, and know that no lie is of the truth."

Tap into this well of understanding within you!

Lord, we invite You to work in us according to your good pleasure. We trust You to reveal and to show us truth. We are willing to let go of any preconceived ideas. We renounce the fear of man; we love Your approval alone. Thank You for depositing such treasure within us ... help us draw it out.

Inexhaustible

... And I ask him that with both feet planted firmly on love, you'll be able to take in with all followers of Jesus the extravagant dimensions of Christ's love. Reach out and experience the breadth! Test its length! Plumb the depths! Rise to the heights! Live full lives, full in the fullness of God.

No Exaggerations!

The queen of Sheba heard about the fame of Solomon. Stories regarding his wisdom and wealth were so amazing that she felt sure they were exaggerated! So, she decided to go and see for herself. Here is part of that story:

"The queen of Sheba heard about Solomon and his connection with the Name of GOD. She came to put his reputation to the test by asking tough questions. She made a grand and showy entrance into Jerusalem--camels loaded with spices, a huge amount of gold, and precious gems. She came to Solomon and talked about all the things that she cared about, emptying her heart to him. Solomon answered everything she put to him - nothing stumped him. When the queen of Sheba experienced for herself Solomon's wisdom and saw with her own eyes the palace he had built, the meals that were served, the impressive array of court officials and sharply dressed waiters, the lavish crystal, and the elaborate worship extravagant with Whole-Burnt-Offerings at the steps leading up to The Temple of GOD, it took her breath away. She said to the king, "It's all true! Your reputation for accomplishment and wisdom that reached all the way to my country is confirmed. I wouldn't have believed it if I hadn't seen it for myself; they didn't exaggerate! Such wisdom and elegance--far more than I could ever have imagined." (1Kings 10:1-7 Message)

Jesus referred to this story saying: *"The queen of the south* shall rise up in the judgment with this generation, and shall condemn it: for she came from the uttermost parts of the earth to hear the wisdom of Solomon; and, behold, a greater than Solomon is here." (Matthew 12:42) If the wealth and wisdom of Solomon could not be adequately described; if it was impossible to exaggerate, how much more impossible is it to exaggerate what we have in Christ. We cannot make too much of Him or what He achieved on our behalf.

What God communicated in Christ was not just another fragment, another portion. No! Christ is the complete and final Word of God. God's entire thought was expressed when the Word became flesh.

I have witnessed so many well-meaning believers waiting for every new word, every new wave, every new prophesy, swept to and fro by every wind of 'new revelation'. What we discover in Christ is not a fashionable 'now' word, but rather the original authentic thought of God!

Paul said it this way in 1 Cor 2: "*We, of course, have plenty of wisdom to pass on ... but it's not popular wisdom, the fashionable wisdom of high-priced experts that will be out-of-date in a year or so. ... It's not the latest message, but more like the oldest—what God determined as the way to bring out his best in us, long before we ever arrived on the scene.* "

It might be fresh in our appreciation or new in our understanding, but God is not busy thinking out a new message every day - everything He wanted to say, was said in absolute clarity in Christ Jesus. We need to wake up to that reality.

Heb 12:25: *If Jesus is the crescendo of God's final utterance, you cannot afford to politely excuse yourself from this conversation.*

Take your lead from Jesus. He is your reference to a complete life. Yesterday is being confirmed today and today mirrors tomorrow. What God spoke to us in Christ is as relevant now as it was in the prophetic past and will always be in the eternal future! (Heb 13:8 Mirror)

He Blew Our Definitions Apart.

"*We don't label people like we used to, with our handy pre-printed tags. We even tried doing this with Jesus, but He blew our definitions apart*" (2 Cor 5:16 The Word on the street translation)

Jesus blew our definitions apart ... and still does. Jesus simply did not fit religious expectations ... and still doesn't. He did not qualify for any of the official religious positions that were available ... yet God highly exalted Him and gave Him a name above every other name. His background was a bit dodgy, too dodgy for some to associate with Him ... yet before Abraham was, He is. His authority was questioned because He did not subject Himself under the 'covering' of any of the groups of His day … yet the Father acknowledged Him and that was all the recognition He needed. The religious structures of His day could not contain Him … and still He does not dwell in temples or institutions made by human hands.

If there was anyone who should have recognised who Jesus really was, it should have been those who dedicated their lives to the study of the prophetic scriptures … yet, being absorbed in interpreting the past and defining their future hope, they missed the present – the greatest event that occurred right in front of their eyes.

John 5:39 *"You have your heads in your Bibles constantly because you think you'll find eternal life there. But you miss the forest for the trees. These Scriptures are all about me!"*

How many precious believers are stuck in the same trap today – busy refining and redefining their doctrine, yet neutralised by a future expectation that contributes nothing to their present encounter with God.

Present Awareness

This past week a few friends came to visit and we had such a thought provoking conversation on how our personal journeys and lives up to this stage, had contributed to our communication of the gospel … or so we thought! It is obvious that if we have shared experiences, such common ground can create opportunity to connect with others. Looking for something you have in common with someone else is a great strategy in making contact or starting a relationship. Sharing parts of your life, your personal journey, can also be a great way of testifying to the love of God and we should never discount the value of an honest account of God's goodness in our lives.

Testimonies are great as a means of pointing towards the substance. However, the substance of our message is more than our personal journeys in life and more than God's personal dealings with us. Ultimately, the substance of our message is an introduction to the person of Christ or our message has no substance at all. This gospel is more than the story of God's involvement in my life so far, or your life so far. God wants to overwhelm us with the reality of His presence to such an extent that the past becomes irrelevant! Even the good memories and the testimonies of God's goodness, can become stale if our awareness of His very present reflection within us, is somehow lost.

There is a place of awareness – Paul called it the surpassing greatness of knowing Christ Jesus my Lord – that makes every other type of knowledge, discussion or perceived wisdom, irrelevant. Yesterday, today and tomorrow do not add or subtract from who He is. God is, long before time as we know it began. We may use the temporal and stories from our lives to point towards Christ, but he will always be greater and better than what the temporal can contain. He is Himself the content of the gospel and as such the gospel is more than stories about Him, it is the power of God unto salvation.

When Jesus prayed one of the last recorded prayers before His certain death, His words were not nostalgic regarding the past nor were they simply focused on the future, but the power of His testimony was found in its relevance to this moment. Hear what He said and notice the immediacy of His thought.

I have given them the glory You have given Me.
May they be one as We are one.
I am in them and You are in Me.
May they be made completely one,
so the world may know You have sent Me
and have loved them as You have loved Me.
Father, I desire those You have given Me
to be with Me where I am.
Then they will see My glory,
which You have given Me
because You loved Me before the world's foundation.
John 17:22-24

When John wrote the letter we know as 1John, he does

not muse on the days gone past, those awesome days when Christ was still in the flesh with them. No. He overflows with excitement about an experience that is present and available to all. He is the same one who wrote: "*There are so many other things Jesus did. If they were all written down, each of them, one by one, I can't imagine a world big enough to hold such a library of books.*" (John 21:25) One would have imagined that he would have spent the rest of his life recording these words and deeds – I mean these are the words and deeds of God manifested in the flesh! Yet, he doesn't! He discovers a greater message than just recording historic facts – introducing his audience into a living present encounter with I AM. (Not 'I used to be', or 'I will be'). He discovered the God who blows our definitions, our doctrines and our structures apart.

There is only one definition of man – Christ!

All the old fashions are now obsolete. Words like Jewish and non-Jewish, religious and irreligious, insider and outsider, uncivilized and uncouth, slave and free, mean nothing. From now on everyone is defined by Christ, everyone is included in Christ. Col 3:9 MSG

This mystery has been kept in the dark for a long time, but now it's out in the open. God wanted everyone, not just Jews, to know this rich and glorious secret inside and out, regardless of their background, regardless of their religious standing. The mystery in a nutshell is just this: Christ is in you, so therefore you can look forward to sharing in God's glory. It's that simple. That is the substance of our Message. We preach Christ, warning people not to add to the Message. We teach in a spirit of profound common sense so that we can bring each person to maturity. To be mature is to be basic. Christ! No more, no less. (Col 1:26-29 MSG)

Christ is in you! What more do you need? There is nothing more! All that can be done is to appreciate more, the reality of Christ in you!

Opening the Window

1John 1:1: "*That which was from the beginning, which we have heard, which we have seen with our eyes, which we have looked upon, and our hands have handled, of the Word of life*"

Hearing (or reading) is but the first step into an experience much greater than what can be captured in words. Our words can simply point towards this experience, but can never capture it. Let me illustrate: Imagine sitting in a hot, humid room with all the windows closed. The air is stale and breathing is unpleasant. Then, someone opens a window and a breeze brings in a fresh fragrance. The cool movement of air revives your body and soon the stale atmosphere is forgotten. This window opens into a space infinitely greater than itself.

This is what God-inspired words do. They simply open

the window for the Spirit or wind of God to blow and bring refreshment. God-inspired words create an opportunity for encounter with God Himself. This encounter is infinitely greater than what can be captured or explained in words. So many of Christian writings are centered on trying to capture this fresh wind. Instead of opening a window, by simply pointing to realities greater than themselves, these formulas and definitions attempt to capture the wind by closing the window. But as soon as the window is closed the wind ceases to be wind; the refreshing that came from it becomes a memory and pretty soon the same stale air fills the room once again.

Read the Word of God with this in mind; read this book with this in mind. These words refer to a reality greater than themselves. The substance is Christ Himself, and the intimacy He has in mind can never be understood by mere words alone; your spirit needs to connect with His. These words simply open a window and point beyond themselves.

Obviously we will use our minds in loving the Lord, but never forget that loving Him with all your heart precedes loving Him with all your mind. Matthew 22:37 *"Jesus said unto him, Thou shalt love the Lord thy God with all thy heart, and with all thy soul, and with all thy mind."*

Paul's Ever Increasing Revelation of Christ

Paul's love affair with Christ was clearly growing throughout his life. If we read His letters in the sequence in which he wrote them, we find that His insight into Christ continues to grow. His focus never gets diversified, rather, he sees more and more of the meaning of all things in Christ.

Lets look at his initial experience of Jesus and how it grew.

Acts 9:3-9: "*But in going, it happened as he drew near to Damascus, even suddenly a light from the heaven shone around him. And he fell to the earth and heard a voice saying to him, Saul, Saul, why do you persecute Me?*

And he said, Who are you, lord? And the Lord said, I am Jesus whom you persecute. It is hard for you to kick against the goads.

And trembling and astonished, he said, Lord, what will You have me to do? And the Lord said to him, Arise and go into the city, and you shall be told what you must do. And the men who journeyed with him stood speechless, indeed hearing a voice but seeing no one. And Saul was lifted up from the earth, his eyes were opened, but he saw no one. But they led him by the hand and brought him into Damascus. And he was three days not seeing, and did not eat or drink"

In a letter to the believers at Corinth, he gives us further insight into this experience. 2Corinthians 4:6 "*For God, who commanded the light to shine out of darkness, hath shined in our hearts, to give the light of the knowledge of the glory of God in the face of Jesus Christ."*

Just as in creation God began it all, so also our encounter with God begins with His initiative. A revelation of Jesus Christ is a gift from God. So much emphasis has been placed on man's decision for Christ; man's faith in Christ; man's repentance. Here we have an example of God's initiative to reveal Himself to man, in this case Paul. Paul's response was based on Jesus' initiative. Paul did not need any teaching on repentance, or how to have faith, or making a quality decision. The revelation of who Jesus really is, was all that was needed to draw the appropriate response from Paul. If, in our declaration of the gospel, we once again make Christ the focus, if we place our confidence in God's ability to reveal Himself rather than placing our confidence in man's faith, we will see genuine conversions as in the case of Paul. Conversions not based on popular Christian formulas, but based on a spontaneous response to 'the light in the face of Jesus Christ'.

We have changed the natural consequences of seeing Jesus into conditions for seeing Him. There are no conditions you can meet for God to reveal Himself to you. You can simply respond to His initiative. Romans 10:20: And Isaiah boldly says, "*I was found by those who were not looking for me; I was revealed to those who were not asking for me.*" Isaiah 65:1 "*I gave access to them that asked not for Me, I was at hand to them that sought*

Me not; I said: 'Behold Me, behold Me', unto a nation that was not called by My name."

God is ready to reveal Himself even to those who do not seek Him! I remember the words of a beautiful song: "You are the rarest of treasures, yet so easy to find"

Paul gives us a further insight in Galatians 1:15,16: *"But when it pleased God, who separated me from my mother's womb, and called me by his grace, to reveal his Son in me."*

How different is Paul's language from so many of today's 'testimonies'. His testimony is not: *"When I made a decision for Christ then He ..."* or *"when I came to repentance then God ...'* No, he has the order completely reversed! He begins with *"when it pleased God...to reveal His son in me"*. He starts with the initiative of God, and his response is not even spoken about as a willful decision - it's just mentioned as a consequence! (Be careful of making the consequences the conditions!)

The gospel is the good news that God took decisive action in Christ to nullify every possible obstacle between Himself and man. He successfully embraced mankind in Christ Jesus. This is the basis of our decision. This emphasis does not by any means take away the response of faith, rather it intensifies it.

In this book you will find the same emphasis: I don't place

much emphasis on how man must respond, or the importance of man's contribution, simply because there are truths of much greater importance. God's initiative, what He did before you were even born, is the focus of this writing. Obviously our response is valuable, but I acknowledge that it is spontaneous and natural if Christ is revealed. My confidence is not in my ability to accurately capture spiritual revelation in words, but rather in God's ability and desire to reveal Himself to you personally. A revelation of Christ is, therefore, the direction these words point to, the window it opens. If I have to teach a person how to respond to such a revelation, that person obviously did not have a revelation of Christ. It is dead religious traditions that need to teach their followers how to respond. An introduction to the living person of Christ needs no artificial protocols.

The light in the face of Jesus Christ is the light that blinded Paul. It is interesting to find this same Paul saying "*While we look not at the things which are seen, but at the things which are not seen: for the things which are seen are temporal; but the things which are not seen are eternal.* "2 Corinthians 4:18

In the three days of natural blindness that followed, Paul started seeing with a clarity beyond his wildest dreams. God began to reveal His Son in him. He saw a reality within himself that was greater than anything outside of himself. Later he wrote: '*So that we henceforth know no one according to flesh; but if even we have known Christ according to flesh, yet now we know him*

30

thus no longer.' This time of natural blindness was obviously also the beginning of seeing spirit realities regarding God and man that remain hidden to those who do not know how to draw revelation from within.

Behold and Be

What we know is that when Christ is openly revealed, we'll see him—and in seeing him, be like him.

There is nothing that has the ability to transform our lives as much as how we hear and what we behold. What we hear determines what we see and we become what we behold. Beholding truth makes us true.

"*That which was from the beginning, that which we have heard, which we have seen with our eyes; that which we have gazed upon, and our hands handled, concerning the word of life*" (1 John 1:1)

Can you see how the tangible experience of God's presence starts with what we hear. There is a natural progression from hearing to seeing, to gazing, to touching.

What we hear

The Word John speaks about is not the latest fashionable 'revelation', but rather that which was from the beginning. In Christ, God's original thought was preserved since the beginning. The destiny of this Word was always to become flesh. This Word cannot be contained in books ... not even sacred books. Paul said it this way: "*We, of course, have plenty of wisdom to pass on to you once you get your feet on firm spiritual ground, but it's not popular wisdom, the fashionable wisdom of high-priced experts that will be out-of-date in a year or so. God's wisdom is something mysterious that goes deep into the interior of his purposes. You don't find it lying around on the surface. It's not the latest message, but more like the oldest—what God determined as the way to bring out his best in us, long before we ever arrived on the scene.*"

(1 Cor 2:6-9 MSG)

Would you agree that the Word that was in the beginning, that was with God and that was God, was not a book but a person? The truths contained within the scriptures point towards The Truth, which is a person, not a book! In Jesus' days there were many who highly revered the scriptures, yet completely missed its message. Jesus said to the religious scholars of His day: "*You have your heads in your Bibles constantly because you think you'll find eternal life there. But you miss the forest for the trees. These Scriptures are all about me! And here I am, standing right before you, and you aren't willing to receive from me the life you say you want.*" (John 5:39,40 MSG) How often still do we hear messages, backed by many scriptural references, filled with formulas and principles yet oblivious to the person - Christ in you. He still desires to find expression, not only in a doctrine or a teaching, however eloquent they may be, but in a person - in you.

This Word is original not invented last week. This Word is eternal, not seasonal. Even before time as we know it, God made up His mind about us. "*... He chose us in Christ before the foundation of the world ...*" (Eph 1:4) Before we did anything to impress or disappoint Him, He knew us, chose us and uniquely identified us in Christ. Christ came to show us what God originally saw in us, that caused Him to take such an interest in us. You were found in Christ long before you were lost in Adam.

How we hear

Jesus said: "*Take care then how you hear, for to the one who has, more will be given, and from the one who has not, even what he thinks that he has will be taken away.*" (Luke 8:18) There is a way of hearing that will enrich you greatly and there is a way of hearing that will rob you.

Prior to this statement Jesus told the parable of the sower to illustrate some of the different ways of hearing. He likens the Word of God to seed ... seed that is received (heard) in different ways and consequently produces different levels of fruitfulness. I want to liken the progression of hearing, seeing, gazing and touching that I mentioned above, to this parable of the sower.

As the sower goes out to sow, some seed falls along the way on a path - it produces no fruit. For me this speaks of casual, careless 'hearing'. The path is not ready for, nor receptive to the seed. I would say that this is a person that never really heard the message.

Then there is the seed that falls among the rocks. There is a bit of good soil there and so the seed does sprout, but because there is no depth it withers quickly. Often, in the excitement of hearing this gospel, the first response is: what shall I do; how do I apply it? People want to move directly from first hearing this good news to trying to change everything around them.

36

However, it is vital to hear in such a way that what you hear starts changing what you see. Otherwise the excitement might be short lived because as soon as you 'see' a contradiction the whole experience withers. This person is at the hearing stage, but has not heard enough to start seeing.

In each of these illustrations there is a progression in the intensity of 'hearing' and a consequent progression in the fruit it produces. The next example is a person who hears and having some depth, they allow the word to sink in, to change the way they see. Because of this, the seed sprouts and begins to bear fruit. Yet they allow other seed, other words to have an equal place in their lives. This Word is not yet the ultimate word in their lives, it has not captured their exclusive attention yet. Consequently, the seed is not as fruitful as it could be.

"*As for that in the good soil, they are those who, hearing the word, hold it fast in an honest and good heart, and bear fruit with patience.*" This is the person who hears and embraces what they hear. This is a way of hearing that captures the persons heart. Embrace this word until you find yourself inescapably embraced by it. The soil does not have to make the seed grow - the seed spouts and grows of its own accord. The soil simply needs to provide an environment for the seed to remain. Jesus once said: "*If you abide in me and my words abide in you, you will bear much fruit*". 'Abide' does not take much effort. It speaks more of rest than activity.

What we have seen and gazed upon.

As we heed this word, as we give our ears, our attention, we'll begin to see. "*which we have seen with our eyes; that which we have gazed upon*". John uses two variations of the word 'see'. The first is 'horaō'.

Strongs defines it as: Properly to stare at, that is, by implication to discern clearly; by extension to attend to.

The second word is 'theaomai' and it is a more intensive form of the first word, meaning: A prolonged form of a primary verb; to look closely at, that is, by implication to perceive.

Again the progression is evident. Look until you see beyond the obvious. Look beyond the surface and allow the true meaning of this word to captivate your attention. Continue to gaze and soon you'll find this word becoming a tangible reality.

There is no method, technique or process that has a greater ability to transform our lives than simply gazing into this mystery, seeing in it the face of our birth, allowing our attention to be captivated by it. Let me be clear. When I speak of being transformed, I do not mean becoming something that you are not. This transformation is a restoration to the original.

And all of us, as with unveiled face, continued to behold as in a mirror the glory of the Lord, are constantly being transformed into His very own image in ever increasing splendor and from one degree of glory to another (2Cor3:18)

But friends, that's exactly who we are: children of God. And that's only the beginning. Who knows how we'll end up! What we know is that when Christ is openly revealed, we'll see him—and in seeing him, become like him. (1 John 3:2-3)

Can you see in these, how 'transformation' is linked to 'beholding'? Once we start seeing the truth of God's opinion of us and excitement fills our hearts, the first response should simply be one of adoration - lets see more; let's look more deeply, let us gaze upon Him. Such adoration will awaken the appropriate response.

Doers of the word, not just hearers.

"But be doers of the word and not hearers only, deceiving yourselves. Because if anyone is a hearer of the word and not a doer, he is like a man looking at his own face in a mirror; for he looks at himself, goes away, and right away forgets what kind of man he was. But the one who looks intently into the perfect law of freedom and perseveres in it, and is not a forgetful hearer but a doer who acts—this person will be blessed in what he does."

The word 'doer' is so much richer than many translations

bring across. It's the same word from which we get 'poet'.

'poiētēs'

a performer; specifically a "poet": - doer, poet.

It speaks of inspired, passionate expression. When this word is declared as it should be, you'll hear much more than 'do's and 'don'ts', you'll see the face of your origin as in a mirror. The secret to the accurate 'doing' of this word is in accurate 'seeing'. It is the one who looks intently and continues to look, that finds inspired expression - expression birthed from what he sees.

With that in mind I translated James 1:25 as follows:

Look and continue to look,

the perfect, complete, and eternal freedom.

Listen; listen intensily;

listen in such a way

that it bursts forth in inspired expression.

Allow what you hear to awaken the poet in you;

allow what you see to awaken the artist in you.

Then act;

act in the full conviction of what you have seen and heard,

and you will will find delight

and affirmation in your action.

Blameless

We are free to approach him with absolute confidence, fully persuaded in our hearts that nothing can any longer separate us from him. We are invited to draw near now! We are thoroughly cleansed, inside and out, with no trace of sin's stains on our conscience or conduct.

The Unnecessary Battle.

Shortly after the trip I wrote of in chapter one, I began to understand more of what my spirit witnessed during that weekend.

During the previous couple of years, my desire for God and search for real relationship with Him, made a few things very clear to me. I began to realise that the greatest obstacles to fellowship with God, were not the obvious culprits that we would like to blame.

I realised that it was not my environment that made intimacy more or less possible - in the greatest discomfort of a dungeon, Paul found an intimacy that caused him to sing praises. The greatest obstacle to intimacy with God was not circumstances, the people around me, Satan or anything else ... the greatest obstacle was my own thinking!

What a battle raged within me, wanting to enjoy Father intimately, yet finding myself doing things that I knew would hinder our fellowship. And so began a story almost as old as mankind. A person desires to do what is right, but the ability to do it, fails him. Sometimes there is a glimmer of hope! A temptation is resisted and an awareness of God's closeness is experienced, but the moment passes. However ignorant this way of thinking sounds, the truth is that multitudes of people are caught up in a rut of trying to earn the favour of God.

Once a person tastes intimacy with the Creator of all things, no other experience outside of this union has any comparable value. It is more addictive than the most potent drug, yet not destructive at all. Inconsistent fellowship is what drives people to a system of trying to earn God's love, thinking that: "The better I am, the more deserving I am of His presence." At the end of all such effort, we come to the same conclusion: My own efforts cannot produce a consistent enjoyment of God. It never has and it never will.

Uninterrupted Fellowship.

While I was lying on my bed one day, asking God to show me the secret of uninterrupted fellowship with Him, I suddenly became aware of His smile over me. That smile explained more to me than all my previous and subsequent studies. I knew He favoured me and saw no obstacle in our union. His smile was not His response to anything I did, or did not do. I became aware of a love so great that nothing would ever be able to change it. Instantly I knew that even if I were to reject this love and live the most rebellious life, He would still love me with this same love.

David expressed it in the following way:
"Is there anyplace I can go to avoid your Spirit?

to be out of your sight?

If I climb to the sky, you're there!

If I go underground, you're there!

If I flew on morning's wings to the far western horizon,

You'd find me in a minute-

you're already there waiting!

Then I said to myself, "Oh, he even sees me in the dark!

At night I'm immersed in the light!"

It's a fact: darkness isn't dark to you;

night and day, darkness and light,

they're all the same to you."

Ps. 139:7-12 MSG

His smile made it clear: I could never avoid His favour. Suddenly, sin was no longer an issue! I was blissfully unaware of anything against me. This awareness of His favour did, unconsciously, more to transform my outer behaviour than any conscious effort of my own part to act 'right'.

Consciousness of sin.

One of the great shortcomings of the first covenant, is that it never completely removed a sin consciousness from man. (Heb 10:2). But what the first covenant could not do, Jesus did! He did not just take our sin upon Himself, so that we could take His righteousness upon ourselves. This is often the idea portrayed, the idea that we wear a cloak of righteousness, but inside we remain as rotten as before. No! Christ BECAME sin, so that we might BECOME the righteousness of God in Him! (2 Cor 5:21). This is the basis upon which my whole self-awareness changes. If the work of Jesus Christ was a success, I can no longer be aware of a sinful, unrighteous person within. I am aware of a righteous, blameless, innocent and clean inner man, in whom God is well pleased! "*So, friends, we can now - without hesitation - walk right up to God, into "the Holy Place." Jesus has cleared the way by the blood of his sacrifice, acting as our priest before God. The "curtain" into God's presence is his body. So let's do it—full of belief, confident that we're presentable inside and out."*

Heb 10:19-22 MSG

How this changes the reality of my daily life is staggering. We don't have to settle for an inconsistent experience where there are moments of awareness of God, soon to be replaced by the awareness of sin. We can now live in the consciousness of our innocence! This awareness might be interrupted from time to time by the reality of sin, but that sin can be dealt within the moment one becomes aware of it. Interruptions to our consciousness of innocence, are now the exceptions to the rule. Understanding makes the awareness of God's presence permanent.

If I am dressed in my dirty gardening clothes, then I would not have a problem if someone asking me to do a dirty job. But if I'm all dressed up in a spotless white outfit, I would not want to go digging around in the garden. If people are continually told what dirty old sinners they are, then groveling in a bit more sin won't seem too bad. It's an awareness of our blameless innocence that makes sin very unattractive.

"*I am not aware of anything against myself*" describes the awareness Paul walked in. 1Cor. 4:4.

This innocence ... this righteousness, is not a goal, but a gift. Neither is it the final destination, but rather the beginning of an adventurous journey. This innocence allows me access into the depths of God. I now have free access to all the Father has.

This awareness of our innocence, is an essential key to discover more of God. Without knowing your righteousness, you will never have the boldness to press into the deep things of God. It is in knowing our Father's favour that we are confident to inquire, to press, and to ask for things that would sound like blasphemy to those who don't know His love.

You are blameless. You are innocent. You are righteous. You are favoured. You are loved. You are all God requires you to be, to pour His love on you. In Christ He reconciled the world to Himself, no longer holding their trespasses against them. He sees no obstacle between Himself and you. There are no reasons for you to, for one more moment, allow a sense of distance or an inferior attitude. Jesus made possible, a life without the consciousness of sin – take it; live it!

What does God say about sin?

A question that often pops up, is how the confession of sin fits with this newfound awareness of our innocence. Let's have a look:

"If we claim to have fellowship with him yet walk in the darkness, we lie and do not live by the truth. But if we walk in the light, as he is in the light, we have fellowship with one another, and the blood of Jesus, his Son, purifies us from all sin. 8If we claim to be without sin, we deceive ourselves and the truth is not in us. If we confess our sins, he is faithful and just and will forgive us our sins and purify us from all unrighteousness." 1 John 1:6-9

So here is a person who claims to have fellowship or intimacy with God, yet walks in darkness. Obviously he deceives himself! Paul had the same experience, where people took the message he preached and came to the completely wrong conclusion, namely: *"Shall we go on sinning so that grace may increase?"* Paul answers: *"By no means"* (Rom 6)

Why would people come to such a conclusion off the back of Paul's preaching? Well, he said things like: *"that God was reconciling THE WORLD to himself in Christ, not counting men's sins against them."* The same world He made - the same world that belongs to Him, is the world He forgave!

However, some saw the generosity of God as an opportunity to continue living in darkness, yet at the same time claiming to have fellowship with God. With Paul we can say: "*By no means is this the conclusion of this gospel.*"

So to these people John says: confess your sin. Confess is the greek word 'homologeō' made up of '*homo*' which means '*the same*' and '*logos*' which is often translated '*word*'. God wants us to say the same about sin as what He says about it. What does He say?

"*This is final: I have deleted the record of your sins and misdeeds. I no longer recall them. (Nothing in God's reference of man, reminds him of sin.) Sins were dealt with in such a thorough manner that no further offerings would ever again be required. Nothing that we can personally sacrifice could add further virtue to our innocence.*" Heb 10:17,18 Mirror

It is the once and for all sacrifice of Christ that is the basis of our confession. Our confession is not a bribe to convince God to forgive us based on how sorry we are. No! There is no merit in anything we can offer! God forgave the world and our confession is to re-align our thinking and our words to conform to what He achieved in Christ.

In Rom 5 Paul says that while we were yet sinners, He reconciled us - embraced us. Awake to God's reality. Aligning our thoughts and confession to His reality will stop the self-deception of saying one thing but living another.

If indeed the Word is true and God has blotted out - removed from His memory - every trace of sin, then there is no reason to involve ourselves in the details of sin. Let's say what He says: "*This is final: I have deleted the record of your sins and misdeeds. I no longer recall them.*" YES!

Identity Revealed

When I consider Your heavens, the work of Your fingers,
The moon and the stars, which You have ordained;
What is man that You take thought of him,
And the son of man that You care for him?

"Jesus replied, 'my testimony is true; for I know where I came from and where I am going'" John 8:14

The knowledge of your origin, the understanding of your identity, is what makes your life real and your convictions true. Understanding your identity is a foundational truth necessary for the construction of other truths.

You did not begin when you were born, nor even when you were conceived. Neither are you simply the product of your ancestry. Even if you could trace your ancestry back - as far back as Adam, that would not reveal who you truly are.

Ephesians 1:4 ".. *He chose us in Him before the foundation of the world, that we should be holy and without blame before Him in love"*

You precede creation! You are older than the Dinasaurs! Before this world was formed you were in Him, and He chose you to become part of creation. Although you are part of creation, your substance is eternal, without beginning and without end. He recognised you in Himself, before creation.

When we speak of that which is eternal, we can't really use words that relate to time and space. Words such as 'begin' make no sense when describing that which is eternal. Yet, for the sake of description we can say that man began in the thought of God.

This is the way our Father operates. Everything has it's origin in His 'Logos' – logic or thought. "In the beginning was the (Logos) Word and the 'Logos' was with God and the 'Logos' was God. "*All things were made by Him and without Him nothing was made that was made ...*" 1 John 1:1,3

His thoughts are not vague, fleeting impressions that have no lasting effect. His thoughts have more substance and permanence than anything you can touch or see. The whole material universe came out of the thoughts of God and at this very moment all creation is sustained, held in existence by His powerful word.

A blueprint can be defined as a detailed construction plan. Throughout the process of construction, it remains the valid reference to the Architects vision. The Father, the Author of life, meticulously planned us. That design remains in Him to this day. That plan remains His unchangeable reference to who you are.

Before any time-related event, God made up His mind about you. Before you did anything to impress or disappoint Him, He decided that you are the focus of His love. Your existence, who you are, was established when God first thought of you. "*To Rebecca, also, a promise was made that took priority over genetics. When she became pregnant by our one-of-a-kind ancestor, Isaac, and her babies were still innocent in the womb—incapable of good or bad—she received a special assurance from God. What God did in this case made it perfectly plain that his purpose is not a hit-or-*

miss thing dependent on what we do or don't do, but a sure thing determined by his decision, flowing steadily from his initiative."
Rom 9 :10-13 MSG

How often do we allow our experiences to teach us who we are? Obviously, we learn from our experiences, but often we try and learn from them, lessons that they are not qualified to teach us. There are no experiences numerous or large enough to contain the revelation of your identity. It can only be received as a gift.

The Father also knew the events that would follow creation. His creation would suffer perversion and wickedness – events that would twist man completely beyond recognition of His original intent. But God's original design, which was conceived in the eternal realm, even before time began, remains unchallenged by time-related events. He knows that time is temporal, and so anything that could be twisted can be untwisted.

What do you refer to, to describe yourself? Is it your family traits, your unique childhood, your achievements? Or maybe you have allowed some tragedy to become the defining event of who you are. There is a more valid reference! If you don't discover that reference, you will allow events to shape and twist you. But when you discover that your identity was established in eternity, no time related event will have the power to deceive you any more.

Whether your experiences confirm or contradict the truth, should have no effect on your persuasion of the truth. When Isaac, the confirmation of Gods promise to Abraham, became too important to Abraham, he had to take Isaac to the altar. Never place more value on the confirmation of the truth than on truth itself.

Come to this conclusion: I am more than the sum total of my experiences. I am greater than all the events in my life joined together. I'm bigger than my biggest disappointment or achievement. I am the image and likeness of God and not a fraction of me, has been revealed!

Another way in which people can define themselves is by what they have gained, or by what they have lost. Pride and regret are both deceptions, designed for the same purpose: to blind man from seeing his true value. Your value is far beyond all the wealth you can attain; a value undiminished by anything you have ever lost.

Beyond Theory.

I remember the time when this truth became a very significant revelation to me. My children were young, about four and six years old. For more than a year I battled to save our business, but the time of reckoning had finally come. All our possessions were repossessed ...

I remember ushering my family into the empty building we used to consider home. Our beds had been left, and in a house with no other furniture, everyone soon dispersed to their rooms.

It was all so surreal. I slowly walked through to what used to be my office. For some reason a single plastic chair and a desk were left behind. A few pieces of stationary were scattered over the floor.

I sat down. I tried to comprehend ... to realise what I had lost. It was more than just possessions. It was my reputation, my dreams for the business etc. Worst of all, I failed my family. As the reality of the situation started to dawn, the heavy weight of depression filled the room. My wife walked in and hugged me. Her words surprised me: "I believe in you", she said, and then walked back to the bedroom since she sensed that I wanted to be alone.

Suddenly the Spirit of God allowed me to perceive what was happening in the spirit-realm. The depression I sensed was more than a feeling, it was a personality – a demonic force, which found an opportune time to attach itself to me. A spirit of depression does not only want to make you feel bad, it wants to kill you.

In the midst of all my confusing thoughts, together with the suggestions whispered to me by this demonic spirit, I heard that calm familiar voice of my Father, and in that moment I knew what to do.

I sat down. I picked up a piece of paper and pen. I leaned back in my chair. I could sense the evil anticipation of the demon peering over my shoulder, expecting me to capture on paper the depressing lies he had been whispering. He had no idea that there was another, much clearer voice to which I gave heed.

I started writing: "*I see our future and it is bright...*" The Spirit of God rose within me, lifting me to heights I never knew possible. I began to prophesy over my family. In the midst of a situation that was the most unlikely place to find inspiration, I found a source of inspiration within me that was unaffected by any outside factors. I discovered a joy not bound to any natural event.

I could sense the unbelief; the shock and horror of the demon who thought he had me exactly were he wanted me, but the tables were turned. I knew that I had depressed the demon so much that he had to leave.

I opened my Bible to Hebrews 10:34 "*..but you even submitted with joy when your property was taken from you, being well aware that you have in your own selves a more valuable possession and one which will remain.*"

I discovered that day that I had within myself a value of such awesome importance, that I could attach all my joy to that value. I discovered what Paul referred to as "*the secret of being content in whatever circumstances I am in*" Phil 4:11,12.

That was a defining moment in which my focus turned from what was around me, to what was within me. I no longer allowed my thoughts to dwell on what I did not have; what I lost; what I did not know. I purposely began to meditate upon the fact that the Creator of the universe was my Father, and He considered me more valuable than any material thing. I began to think about what I did have; what I did know, and soon after that, restoration began.

Although that story had an amazing ending, it is not relevant to this writing. What is important is to realise that God delights in being our deliverer. He restored to us so much more than what was stolen.

The conclusion is: Do not allow any event, whether success or failure to define you. Realise that God has invested Himself in you. No experience is big enough to define you - you are the image and likeness of God.

Your Creation

So much is revealed concerning us in the account of creation.

We don't have to guess at what ingredients were used for our 'construction'. Our creation is the event in which God gave expression to His thoughts concerning us.

A common understanding of the word 'creation' is making something out of nothing. It is true that the physical universe was created and God did not use any pre-existent physical substance to do it, but He did use a substance. The substance is called 'LOGOS'.

Let's look a bit closer at the word 'Logos' which is translated 'word' in the New Testament. We also get our English words 'logic' and 'thought' from this word, logos. Logos, however, denotes more than just a thought but also denotes the expression of that thought. Logos includes the motive, the thought, the reasoning or development of that thought and finally, the expression and communication of that thought.

And so, God's thoughts concerning man went beyond a silent plan within Him. He expressed those thoughts when He spoke man into existence. His words were the summary, the conclusion of all that He dreamed concerning man.

What He thought and said are not great mysteries lost through the eons of time. He made sure that they were accurately recorded, so that we could know His original intent.

What are you made of?

The first and most authoritative description of man: "*Let us make man in Our image and Our likeness*".

It follows the same pattern of all the other creative acts such as: "*Let the water bring forth living creatures*" and "*Let the earth bring forth vegetation*" etc. A more literal translation would be: "*Water, bring forth living creatures*" and "*Earth, bring forth vegetation*"

God speaks to the substance from which He wants to make or create the new substance and causes it to bring forth the new creation.

So to whom was God speaking when He said, "*Let us make man in Our image and Our likeness*". I believe He spoke to Himself saying: "*US, bring forth man in Our Image and Our Likeness.*" He spoke to the substance from which man would be made – Himself. He defines man … with a definition so broad that we could never find its boundaries. If you are able to define God (His image and likeness), only then will you be able to define man. There is so much to be said about this! There is a part of man, which is eternal, having no beginning and no end. It is a quality inherent in the substance we were made of – God!

Gen 2:7 gives further insight into what actually happened:

"God formed man from the dust of the earth and breathed into his nostrils the breath of life".

It is the very breath that God breathed into man that is the essence of man. What is this creative breath He breathed into man? It is the words He spoke in chapter 1: 26.

Let's imagine the actual event: God forms the body of man. He leans over and picks up this lifeless form. Then He speaks to the substance from which man is made – Himself: "Us, bring forth man. Our image, Our likeness." The very words He speaks are the breath that transfers man from the inside of God into this body. God reproduces, and man becomes a living being.

Gen 1:28 *"And God blessed them ..."* The word blessed (bawrak) is defined as an act of adoration such as kneeling. Man's very first experience was the overwhelming display of God's favour and adoration! The desire within man to worship God was birthed by this experience of God's adoration – the only appropriate response is to reflect back the adoration He gives. 1John 4:19 *"We love Him because He first loved us".* Man alone can appreciate and respond to His love on this level.

To summarise: Paul discovered the awesome truth that we were in Christ BEFORE the foundation of the world. We were before the world was. We became part of creation, but creation is not our beginning for we are eternal beings, without beginning and without end. This means that we can never allow temporal events to define us. God, our Father, defined us as His very own image and likeness. Temporal events can confirm or contradict this truth, but they can never change it.

The God-kind

Because both he who carried out the act of rescue and those whom he rescued and restored to innocence originate from the same source, he proudly introduces them as members of his immediate family.

We have discovered such precious truths about mankind. We originate in the heart and mind of God. Before creation, we were in Him. God Himself is the substance from which man was made. The most authoritative description of man came from God Himself. He described us as His own image and His own likeness. God adores man; He enjoys our company!

Further on in the scriptures in Psalm 8 and Heb 2 we read that man was made '*a little lower than the angels*' in some translations, or '*a little lower than God*' in other translations. The original does refer to God rather than angels. However it does still seem like a contradiction or at least an inaccuracy. I asked the Lord about this seeming contradiction at one stage: "Were we made in the God-class or a little lower?" I then went and looked at the wording in Psalm 8. Interestingly it never refers to man being 'created' lower, but rather 'made lower' as in demoted. The Hebrews account makes it even clearer by adding the words: "*made lower for a little while*". So this was a temporary demotion. Man was subjected to a place of inferiority for a while through his inclusion in the first Adam. Thank God for the last Adam that brought that state and race of being to an end!

I can hear the many objections racing through people's minds when they are presented with the thought of exact likeness to God. I had the same objections for very good reasons. There are obviously many qualities that God possesses that I don't. He is omnipresent (present everywhere), I am not. He is omnipotent (having all power), I am not, etc. Much later He inspired a piece of writing that gives us such clear insight into His being:

If I speak the languages of men and of angels, but do not have love, I am a sounding gong or a clanging cymbal. If I have prophecy, and understand all mysteries and all knowledge, and if I have all faith, so that I can move mountains, but do not have love, I am nothing. (1 Cor 13)

These words reveal something about the God of love, namely: it is not His infinite knowledge or intellect, referred to as His omniscience, that is His most essential characteristic. Neither is it His limitless power, known as His omnipotence, that makes Him who He is. Love is at the core of who God is!

It is man's capacity to receive, to produce and to exchange the same quality of love that flows within God that makes us the God-kind, the God-class of being.

A question that follows close on the heels of these discoveries is: Are we equal to God?

Well, it depends on what we mean by equality. The basic definition of 'equality' is to share the same qualities. The more that is shared in common the greater the degree of equality. Our understanding of equality only becomes clear when we understand the word 'fellowship'.

The word 'fellowship' means to share things in common. The more you share in common, the higher the degree of fellowship or intimacy.

Our equality with God exists only within the environment of fellowship. We cannot be equal to, and separate from God, because separation is the very opposite of sharing all things in common. This equality is only possible in unity. John 15:5 - "*I am the vine, you are the branches*". The same life-giving sap flows through both – the branch shares the same life as the vine as long as it is in union with it. So, when we talk about man being in the God-class of being, there can be no suggestion that man is god in and by himself. No! It is in union with Him that we are partakers of the Divine nature. (2Pet1:4).

John 10:30 "*I and the Father are one!*" Is this an exclusive statement that only Jesus could make?

John 17:22,23 "*And I have given them the glory which You have given Me, that they may be one, even as We are one, I in them, and You in Me, that they may be made perfect in one; and that the world may know that You have sent Me and have loved them as You have loved Me.*"

One with God! One with the Father; One with the Son; One with His Spirit! The same union that Jesus enjoys with the Father is our portion! The same love, the same oneness, the

66

same perfection. Whatever Jesus said about His relationship with the Father, we can say! It was this very consciousness of His union with the Father that got Jesus into such trouble with the religious leaders.

"*I and the Father are one! Then the Jews took up stones again to stone Him. Jesus answered them, I have shown you many good works from My Father; for which of these do you stone Me? The Jews answered Him, saying, We do not stone you for a good work, but for blasphemy, and because you, being a man, make yourself God. Jesus answered them, Is it not written in your Law, "I said, You are gods?" If He called those gods with whom the Word of God was, and the Scripture cannot be broken, do you say of Him whom the Father has sanctified and sent into the world, You blaspheme, because I said, I am the Son of God?*"

John 10:30,36

Jesus was accused of making man equal with God. How did He respond? He did not deny this charge! He confirms their accusation by quoting Psalm 82:6.

1John 1:1-3 "*That which was from the beginning, which we have heard, which we have seen with our eyes, which we have looked upon, and our hands have handled, concerning the Word of Life, (for the Life was revealed, and we have seen it and bear witness, and show to you the everlasting Life, who was with the Father and was revealed to us), that which we have seen and heard we declare unto you, so that you also may have fellowship with us. And truly our fellowship is with the Father and with His Son Jesus Christ."*

This quality of fellowship, this intimacy is not possible between beings on different levels. You might have a measure of relationship with a cat, but it has its limits. God did not imagine a pet, when He imagined you. His desire was for nothing less than a being in His own class, on His own level. Father intended a relationship without limits, and therefore conceived a being that is compatible with His own infinite self.

Phi 2:5-8 *"Let this mind be in you, which was also in Christ Jesus: Who, being in the form of God, thought it not robbery to be equal with God: But made himself of no reputation, and took upon him the form of a servant, and was made in the likeness of men: And being found in fashion as a man, he humbled himself, and became obedient unto death, even the death of the cross."*

Paraphrased: Have the same attitude that Jesus had. He knew that He was equal to God, and this assurance gave Him the confidence to be a servant without an inferiority complex.

We don't have to justify or nervously defend this position of equality, for we have not promoted ourselves to this position. He made us this way! This awareness does not give us a superior attitude, but it is the very knowledge that sets us free to serve others with complete abandonment.

The original deception was a suggestion that man was created less than the image and likeness of God; that God was withholding something from us, and that through some process we could attain it. The truth was that man was already like God and He provided a way for us to partake of His very life — the Tree of life. God was not withholding anything! Neither was equality with Him a thing to be grasped or attained. All that was and is left for man to do is awaken to the fact that we are like Him.

I, in righteousness, I see Thy face; I am satisfied, in awaking, with Thy form (or likeness)! (Psalm17:5)

Untamed

Forget about trying to find His plan for your life - your life is His plan! Neither you location nor your timing matters - He has dawned His eternal day. You are His moment; you are His location!

"... worship the Father neither here at this mountain nor there ... It's who you are" John 4:21-23 MSG

Have you ever witnessed a wild animal in its natural environment? A tame lion simply does not have the presence of a wild one. A wild lion has an attitude, an assurance in its walk. The unrestricted environment, and the untamed nature of the animal complement one another. To tame such a creature, and remove it from its environment, is to rob it of its identity.

Acts 17:28 "*For in Him we live, and move, and have our being.*" God Himself is the natural environment in which man is to live! What an unrestricted environment for the expressive nature He gave us.

Speaking about Jesus, Paul says the following: "*So spacious is he, so roomy, that everything of God finds its proper place in him without crowding.*" and "*Everything of God gets expressed in him*" and "*for in him dwells all the fullness of the Godhead bodily*" (Col 1:19 ; 2:9) The physical body of Jesus did not restrict God. In fact He found full expression in this man. Man is the natural environment that God designed for Himself, as the place where He would live and move and have His being!

To try to domesticate and restrict this relationship is completely unnatural. The relationship He has in mind with us is authentic, untamed and wild!

How we freshly appreciate the wonder of God becoming flesh, as we recognise His likeness in one another. To recognise the Father in one another has always been His idea. To recognise Him, need not be some spectacular event or some visible glow upon your head. We simply need to see from His point of view, for He recognises His own image and likeness within each man. Have you ever wondered what God's mirror looks like? When God looks at you, He looks into a mirror – He recognises Himself in you! Jesus was a person so much like us, so ordinary, that the Pharisees had to pay someone to point Him out. Yet He said that if anyone saw Him they saw the Father. We do not need a new event, a more spectacular demonstration, to recognise the Father – we simply need a new appreciation of how He chose to reveal Himself. He chose man! His ultimate intention was never for His Word to be captured in a book, a doctrine, but to become flesh – to be expressed in human form. A blank piece of paper makes no contribution to the message written by the author – as living epistles we can only let God, the author and finisher of our faith, write whatever He determined to write through our lives.

You are designed for intimacy with the Father. There is nothing difficult or unnatural about it. This intimacy is not limited to a venue, or dependant on a specific environment. It is not limited to an event or a specific time. God's chosen moment of encounter is always now. Neither is this relationship in any way related to your contribution! Jesus did not say to the woman at the well that once she gives Him a cup of water, then He will take her contribution, and multiply it, and make it a fountain in her. Before she gave Him anything Jesus said: "*If you knew the generosity of God and who I am, you would be asking me for a drink, and I would give you fresh, living water.*" If you know the generosity of God, you will never again be conscious of your own contribution!

Jesus' last words on the cross were not: "I've done my part, given my 50% - now I'm waiting for your contribution!" No! He did not even give 90% - waiting for our 10%. Hear His words thunder in your heart: "*It is finished!*"

Jesus quoted from Ps 22: "*Posterity shall serve Him; they shall tell of the Lord to the next generation. They shall come and shall declare His righteousness to a people yet to be born--that He has done it [that it is finished]!*"

What boldness - we can shout it to a generation not yet born: He has done it! Its a done deal!

At another stage, when Jesus taught how to react to the reality of daily needs, He advised us to look at the birds that neither sow nor reap! The Father's provision has nothing to do with your contribution! Jesus taught on sowing and reaping at another time, but in this context He advised us to rather place our focus on the Father's goodness than on our contribution!

John 4:11 -15: *Jesus answered, "If you knew the generosity of God and who I am, you would be asking me for a drink, and I would give you fresh, living water."*

The woman said, "Sir, you don't even have a bucket to draw with, and this well is deep. So how are you going to get this 'living water'? Are you a better man than our ancestor Jacob, who dug this well and drank from it, he and his sons and livestock, and passed it down to us?"

Jesus said, "Everyone who drinks this water will get thirsty again and again. Anyone who drinks the water I give will never thirst--not ever. The water I give will be an artesian spring within, gushing fountains of endless life."

The woman said, "Sir, give me this water so I won't ever get thirsty, won't ever have to come back to this well again!"

Jesus offers more than any religious practise could ever offer. Religion relies on its followers remaining needy, so that they will continually come to it for some relief. Jesus offers more than just an occasional satisfying experience, but one that overflows without interruption. The relationship He has in mind frees us from the need to continually go somewhere to experience it.

John 4:20,21,24:

"Well, tell me this: Our ancestors worshiped God at this mountain, but you Jews insist that Jerusalem is the only place for worship, right?"

"Believe me, woman, the time is coming when you Samaritans

will worship the Father neither here at this mountain nor there in Jerusalem.....

But the time is coming--it has, in fact, come--when what you're called will not matter and where you go to worship will not matter. "It's who you are and the way you live that count before God."

Our encounter with the Father is no longer limited to "*here or there*". There is no place that has an advantage in terms of containing more of God. Where you are does not matter! It is who you are! You are His chosen location – you are the Father's address on earth. We can also take off the limitations of waiting for a time to come and realise that "*it has, in fact, come* ".

Let us summarise what we have said so far about our intimacy with the Father:

- it is not limited to our contribution.
- it is not restricted to a place, a venue or a specific environment.
- it is not confined to specific times.

His time is NOW. Just like you can't live on the memory of your last meal nor the expectation of a future meal, you were not designed for mental encounter with Father, but a real partaking of His substance.

You are His venue. Who you are, is the only environment

necessary for encounter. Remember, this intimacy is with 'I AM' not with 'I USED TO BE' or ' I AM GOING TO BE' He only knows of one appropriate time and that is NOW. God gave us a huge clue in His name concerning the time-context in which He wants to encounter us. 'I AM' is only available in this moment.

Mat 17:1-5 *Six days later, three of them saw that glory. Jesus took Peter and the brothers, James and John, and led them up a high mountain. His appearance changed from the inside out, right before their eyes. Sunlight poured from his face. His clothes were filled with light. Then they realised that Moses and Elijah were also there in deep conversation with him.*

Peter broke in, "Master, this is a great moment! What would you think if I built three memorials here on the mountain--one for you, one for Moses, one for Elijah?"
While he was going on like this, babbling, a light-radiant cloud enveloped them, and sounding from deep in the cloud a voice: "This is my Son, marked by my love, focus of my delight. Listen to him."

"This is a great moment!" was Peter's response to this awesome event. Then he suggests doing, what so many religious organisations have done: build a structure to try and capture the moment. But Jesus ignores his babbling, for Jesus knew the time would come when Peter would realise that such awesome moments are accessed from within.

Later, Peter wrote about this experience in the following way:

For John, James and I the prophetic word is fulfilled beyond doubt; we heard this voice loud and clear from the heavenly realm while we were with Jesus in that sacred moment on the mountain. For us the appearing of the Messiah is no longer a future promise, but a fulfilled reality; now it's your turn to have more than a second hand, hear-say testimony, take my word as one would take a lamp at night, the day is about to dawn for you in your own understanding; when the morning star appears, you no longer need the lamp, this will happen shortly on the horizon of your hearts...
2 Pet 1:18-19 Mirror Translation

Can you see how Peter's perception of this event changed? He no longer longed for it as a great moment that had to be captured. He now discovered a more sure word or confirmation within himself. A great moment with God is no longer isolated to some special place or time. The indwelling presence of God is the light, is the moment, is all we could ever hope for. You are His chosen 'structure', His mobile temple, and He desires no other structure as His dwelling.

Let us now take a step deeper. The Father does not intend your worship and adoration to be focussed on Him externally. He wants you to realise, recognise, and appreciate that the very qualities you adore in Him, He reproduced in you!

John 12:20-24: *"There were some Greeks in town who had come up to worship at the Feast. They approached Philip, who was from Bethsaida in Galilee: "Sir, we want to see Jesus. Can you help us?"*

Philip went and told Andrew. Andrew and Philip together told Jesus.

Jesus answered, "Time's up. The time has come for the Son of Man to be glorified.

"Listen carefully: Unless a grain of wheat is buried in the ground, dead to the world, it is never any more than a grain of wheat. But if it is buried, it sprouts and reproduces itself many times over."

Jesus was not impressed with people who simply came to adore or worship Him. He had a much higher ambition and that was to unleash the image and likeness of God in man! He came to unveil God's authentic thought about man, to restore man to the image and likeness for which He designed us; to break the dormancy of the DNA of God that remained hidden, in lifeless seed form, in each man; to remind mankind that we belong, that we have the image of our owner stamped upon our being.

To focus and magnify your own shortcomings and faults brings no honour to God. How is a father honoured in the dishonouring of his children? The Father's greatest delight is when His children discover and give expression to the qualities He gave birth to in us.

"Ascribe ye greatness unto our God. He is the Rock, his work is perfect" Deut. 32:3,4

Union

When reading the New Testament I have found that there is an ever present theme throughout these writings; an awareness of this awesome truth that God has made His abode in us. It's an awareness of union with Him that is so rich and strong that it frightens many who read it. There is nothing in their writing that tries to explain away this union or justify distance. Those who are frightened by these truths have spent much energy and theological thought on trying to describe the separation that remains between us and God; trying to find methods of differentiating between us and God. Any explanation that brings an awareness of distance does not share in the same spirit which we find in the N.T. The New Testament writings overflow with a rich awareness that God has restored the union He always desired. Here are a few of those phrases:

John 17:11,22,23: *"… that they may be one, even as we are one … The glory that you have given me I have given to them, that they may be one even as we are one, I in them and you in me, that they may become perfectly one, so that the world may know that you sent me and loved them even as you loved me."*

Gal. 2:20: *"I no longer live, but Christ lives in me, and the life that I now live in the flesh I live by the faithfulness of the Son of God, who loved me and gave himself for me."*

Col. 3:2,3: *"Keep your minds on things that are above, not on things that are on the earth. For you have died, and your life is hidden with Christ in God."*

Eph. 3:19: *"And to know the love of Christ, which passeth knowledge, that ye might be filled with all the fullness of God."*

1Cor. 6:17: *"But he that is joined unto the Lord is one spirit."*

1John 1:3: *"That which we have seen and heard declare we unto you, that ye also may have fellowship with us: and truly our fellowship is with the Father, and with his Son Jesus Christ."*

Col. 2:9, 10: *"For in him dwelleth all the fullness of the Godhead bodily. And ye are complete in him"*

2 Peter 1:4: *"through which He has given to us exceedingly great and precious promises, so that by these you might be partakers of the divine nature"*

These pages overflow with a consciousness of our union with God; an awareness of such intimacy that we are no longer able to differentiate between His spirit and our spirit. They make no attempt to explain their statements in a way that would allow any knowledge of distance. The fellowship they speak of, is not some inferior acquaintance of a transcendent God that lowers Himself to our level, rather, it is the glorious reality of God raising us to His level and transforming us into His image to enjoy a union of equal quality.

I can no longer think of myself in isolation; I am no longer an individual; I am a union. I have lost myself in this love affair. In beholding Him I have found my true self; my one-with-God self.

There is only one possible limitation that remains and that is limiting our appreciation of these truths. The moment one recognises and appreciates that Father is as close to you as the tongue in your mouth and the heart in your chest, that appreciation unlocks the awareness of union.

Romans 10:8: " ... *The word that saves is right here, as near as the tongue in your mouth, as close as the heart in your chest. It's the word of faith that welcomes God to go to work and set things right for us. This is the core of our preaching.*"

To Know Him

To know Him is simple,
no rituals to hinder.
To know Him is simple,
no levels through which to enter.

To love Him is easy,
no reason to draw back.
To love Him is easy,
no consciousness of lack.

To reach for Him and find Him
is closer than you may think.
To reach for Him and find Him
'Tis within you, this link.

To see Him close your eyes,
awaken to that inner light.
To see Him look within,
His vision will ignite.

It's easy, It's simple:
Within you, right now,
reach for Him, find Him,
love Him and know Him, now!

Christ -
Light, Life, Love

God delights in revealing Himself. He overflows with life. He brims over with love. He bursts forth with light. At the very core of who God is, is this urgency to express Himself; to manifest Himself; to demonstrate His love.

Light

John describes God as light, life, and love. God is light and in Him is no darkness at all. His light is not just any light, it is absolute light. Darkness cannot understand or overcome it. Light is not a passive quality - it's dynamic, explosive. Light desires to shine! This is God; He desires to reveal Himself. He is not withdrawn, un-knowable and hidden. He is light, and He desires to enlighten every man with the knowledge of His favour. While Paul was hunting down the followers of Jesus Christ, Jesus revealed Himself to Paul. Later Paul writes about the God who reveals Himself to those who do not seek Him! He makes His sun to shine on the evil and the good. It is in His nature to reveal Himself; it has nothing to do with your ability to attain revelation, it has everything to do with His desire to reveal Himself, independent of you deserving or not deserving it!

John 1:4: "*In him was life; and the life was the light of men.*"

John 1:9: "*He was the true Light which enlightens every person coming into the world.*"

The life Jesus lived, is the light of man. His life reveals who mankind really is. Jesus was not just an example for man, but of man! Light allows us to appreciate the beauty and value of something. Darkness covers and hides things to such an extent that we are not even certain of its existence - but when light comes, we suddenly see the reality of what darkness denied. Light persuades us firstly of the existence of the object and then reveals its beauty.

Life

God is life, and in Him is no death at all! The Greek word for this God-kind of life is 'Zoe'. It has the meaning of absolute life in it. Jesus spoke about this life as abundant life. At another time He described it as a spring of living water bursting forth from within you. Again, this is no passive quality. God is not passive; He brims over with life. He lives abundantly, and desires to share this abundant life. His life is so expansive and so full of goodness that He simply has to share it.

When the life within a fruit tree becomes more than what it needs to sustain itself, it produces fruit. This fruit contains the seed for another tree. This abundance of life spilled over and reproduced itself. It is this abundance of life, in God, that spilled over and produced man. The glorious life He enjoyed was more than He needed for Himself. The desire to share this extravagance, resulted in creation.

Love

God is love. Love's greatest need is to give. This is no passive love either, but a love that manifests itself. He demonstrated His love toward us, in that while we were at enmity against Him, He reconciled us to Himself! While the world was still spitting in His face and breathing out hatred against Him, He kissed the world and declared that their trespasses would no longer be held against them. This is a love so great that it could not wait for man to approach, but took the initiative to embrace us while we were still hostile.

God's Expressive Nature.

We so often limit our perceptions to our own points of view. We see the love of God only within the context of our own need. But it is not so much our need for His love that caused Him to reach out to us, as it is His own desire to simply love. It is not just the intensity of the darkness we are in, that motivates Him to bring light. It is simply His nature to shine forth.

God delights in revealing Himself. He overflows with life. He brims over with love. He bursts forth with light. At the very core of who God is, is this urgency to express Himself; to manifest Himself; to demonstrate His love. The whole of the universe is testimony to His enormous desire and ability to express Himself. Every galaxy, every plant, every animal is a unique manifestation of His imagination. But ultimately a person wants to express Himself through a personality and that's why God made you!

Love needs to give. Light's nature is to shine. Life reproduces. These are the characteristics of God; these are His essential qualities. This expressive nature of God gave birth to His ultimate plan and purpose: He designed a vehicle, a being through which He would accurately and completely express Himself! He preserved that design in Christ. You are part of that design! The Word describes His eternal purpose as a body through which He would live; a living temple which He would fill Himself and dwell in; a kingdom of light and love in which He would put away all contradiction. All these descriptions testify to an expressive God. His eternal purpose is to fully express Himself. In Christ the fullness of the Godhead dwells in a bodily form and you find your completeness in Him.

Col. 2:9-11: *"Everything of God gets expressed in him, so you can see and hear him clearly. You don't need a telescope, a microscope, or a horoscope to realise the fullness of Christ, and the emptiness of the universe without him.*

When you come to him, that fullness comes together for you, too. His power extends over everything.

Entering into this fullness is not something you figure out or achieve. It's not a matter of being circumcised or keeping a long list of laws. No, you're already in--insiders--not through some secretive initiation rite but rather through what Christ has already gone through for you, destroying the power of sin "

In 1 Corinthians 12:12, we see that Christ is no longer a

single individual but made up of many parts, namely: you and me! So what do I mean when I refer to Christ as God's ultimate design? The expressive qualities of God - light, life , love - needed a way of expression. The way, the environment, the body that He designed that enables such an expression, is Christ. "*Everything of God gets expressed in him*" And this is worth repeating: Christ no longer refers to a single individual, but to the many. God desired you as part of His unique expression.

Hebrews 10:5: "*Therefore when He comes into the world, He says, "Sacrifice and offering You did not desire, but You have prepared a body for Me."*

In Jesus, we see God expressing Himself. Both in the life He lived, and in the death He died, God finds full expression. When Jesus heals, God heals. When Jesus spoke, God spoke. When Jesus died, we see the heart of God ... willing to suffer on our behalf. Shortly after the resurrection, we see Peter and John healing the cripple man. God continues to live in and through people! Even more marvelous than the healing of the cripple man, is the fact that God continues to live through people. The fact that Jesus is no longer here in a physical body, does not mean that God is no longer here in a physical body! He is! He lives in and through those who let Him. He disappeared from our sight, that we might return to our hearts and find Him there.

Christ -
The Revelation

"... for if any man hears this word, he is like a man that sees
the face of his birth as in a mirror ..."

James 1:23

The revelation of Jesus Christ.

What Jesus accomplished and revealed through His life, death, and resurrection can never be exaggerated or exhausted. Eph. 2:7: "*so that in the ages to come He might show the exceeding riches of His grace in His kindness toward us through Christ Jesus.*"

God sees the work and revelation of Christ as being so rich, that He plans to use all of time to come to demonstrate, and further reveal its true meaning. This is not just another doctrinal subject to be neatly categorised and added to all the other subjects. This is the revelation that gives meaning and perspective to all other revelations. Without this revelation, all other knowledge remains in the class of human speculation and philosophical guessing.

Because this thought is so broad, I want us to focus on just one part of it in this chapter, namely: What Christ revealed concerning man. When God's Word became man, He also became God's final Word about man. The most essential ingredient of what Christ revealed is the true nature and identity of God and man. "*It's in Christ that we find out who we are and what we are living for. Long before we first heard of Christ and got our hopes up, He had his eye on us, had designs on us for glorious living ...*" Eph 1:11 (MESSAGE)

God became man…. the most awesome thing about it is not that He could lower Himself to the level of man, but that He could elevate man to His own class and nature. He declared through this act that mankind had the capacity to be partakers of His divine nature. Eph. 4:13: " *until we all attain to the unity of the faith and of the knowledge of the Son of God, to mature manhood, to the measure of the stature of the fullness of Christ.*" Christ became the measure of man. To become a fully developed man, means nothing less than standing in the full measure of Christ - the exact representation of the character of God.

A child has all the bones, muscles and ligaments of an adult. They just need to develop. Man, created in the image and likeness of God, was given a wake-up call in Christ to be all that God intended man to be. By an open display of what it meant to be a man in fellowship with God, He appealed to every man's conscience. We recognise in Him, what we inherently know about ourselves.

When people stood in amazement at what He did, He immediately pointed to them, and told them that they could do it too. He never allowed people to put him on a pedestal, to be adored as a unique individual, far removed from what mere men could ever become. He always included others, lifting them to His own level and explaining that what He did and who He was, was equally available to them. Listen to His words - catch His attitude: "*The works I do, you will do also, and greater works than these"*, *"Just as the Father sent me, I send you."*, *" that they all may be one, as You, Father, are in Me, and I in You, that they also may be one in Us"*. His words are inclusive, not exclusive. His vision was to awaken the same divine life in us, to be the first-born among many brethren, the first-fruits of a great harvest of men and women just like Him! He was not only an example for us, but of us. Jesus Christ – the anointed one – the one who fulfilled the task that He was anointed for - to restore relationship between God and man. He is the revelation of your true identity. *"And then take on an entirely new way of life--a God-fashioned life, a life renewed from the inside and working itself into your conduct as God accurately reproduces His character in you."* (Eph 4:22-24 Message)

As He is, even so are we in this world! Whenever Christ is revealed, we are co-revealed with Him in glory (1Jo 4:17, Col 3:4) He never reveals Himself in isolation. When you see Him, you see yourself; your true self. If your experience does not line up with this revelation, it's because you forgot who you really are. But if you continue to look intensely, and do not forget your true identity, your life and actions will align themselves to what you see. No contradiction can continue when you refuse to agree with what it suggests. No lie can continue when you purposely look at truth.

Your life, who you really are, is preserved in Christ (Col 3:3). As you set your focus and determine not to think of yourself in any other way than what is revealed in Christ, you discover an inexhaustible source of revelation there - revelation about Him and you, you and Him, seeing Him in a mirror until you cannot distinguish between Him and you. Then you exclaim with Paul: *"he who is joined to the Lord is one spirit with Him."*

This is central to the gospel. We cannot think of Jesus Christ, without thinking of the task He accomplished in revealing God and man. So I cannot think of Him without thinking of man – and I cannot think of man without thinking of Him. He revealed man and now men who grasp that revelation, reveal Him.

Paul realised too, that the revelation of Christ, separated him from his natural genealogy Gal 1:15,16 *"But when it pleased God, who separated me from my mother's womb, and called me by his grace, to reveal his Son in me...."*

The truth about you is so much greater than what can be perceived in the natural. You came from God. Our Father valued us even when we did not recognise Him. He lovingly sent His own Son as His final call for us to return to Him again. Let us respond to the greatness of our God – The Rock. (Deut. 32:3,4) Acknowledge that His work (that includes you) is perfect! Ponder the rock from which you were cut (Isaiah 51:1). Know that our Father is the substance from which you were made.

Christ - The Fulness of Time

There is nothing in your future that can add anything to you! "…the world, life, death, the present, the future—all of it is yours…" *1 Cor 3:22 MSG.*

Therefore you can remove the focus of every expectation you ever had based on a future date, and instead place it on the one who is within you. The greatest gift the future holds is the unveiling of the reality within you – Christ!

There is a singular event in time that gives meaning to all other time. It is only within this one event that all other events can find purpose. Although this happened before you were born, it has a greater claim on you than your own personal past.

Whether you are aware of it or not, this event affects you. In fact it's all about you. Paul refers to it as the fullness of time (Eph. 1:10); he describes it as the singular event that has consequences for all of mankind throughout all ages; an achievement that occurred once and included all.

Within this one person, God spoke His complete and final word to, and regarding man. A message of such weight obviously needs to be communicated in the clearest way possible. The only being in which He could accurately express Himself was man. And so ".. *the Word became flesh and dwelt among us..*"

All of scripture points to Him.

The Bible is not a combination of many lessons concerning many subjects, although, if that is all you are looking for, it will most probably be all you will find. The message contained within it is much more. The words simply point to a reality greater than the words themselves - to a person and what He accomplished.

98

"You got your degrees in the sacred books, PhD's in books about the sacred books, and you're convinced they'll get you into heaven. But for all the points you score - you miss the Point: it's all about me! It's jam-packed with huge stomping clues about me. But you can't admit it, 'cos then you'd have to ask me for the limitless life you want." John 5:39,40 The Street Bible

After Jesus' death and resurrection, He joined a conversation with two disciples who did not recognise Him at that moment. The content of His conversation was:

Luke 24:27: *"And beginning at Moses and all the prophets, he expounded unto them in all the scriptures the things concerning himself."*

Luke 24:45: *"He went on to open their understanding of the Word of God, showing them how to read their Bibles this way."*

Our study of the scriptures will remain as dim and veiled as the religious leaders' understanding of Jesus was, if we do not see everything through this one event that happened in this one person - Jesus.

The scriptures are similar to a message which is encrypted with a password. The words and sentences might seem to have meaning, but their true meaning can only be discovered when they are 'decrypted'. In other words the password becomes the formula that gives every word its true meaning. Jesus is the key, the essential part of God's message that gives all other scriptures their true meaning.

This focus, on this one event, is not just an adoration of a historic achievement. When God identified Himself with man, in the most powerful way possible – by becoming a man, He thereby gave us the opportunity to be identified with Him – to find our true identity in Him.

All of scripture is about Jesus, the Christ, and all of Jesus is about you! He came as God's call to you, to remember your origin and return.

Let's look at some of the Old Testament realities that changed with the coming of Jesus. The animal sacrifices ceased because Christ fulfilled all that they pointed to. (Heb. 9:19-26) His sacrifice became the final and unrepeatable act that forever dealt with the sin problem. The priesthood and the rituals that stood between God and those who worshipped Him, ceased. (Heb. 7:23,24).

We now all have an open invitation to boldly come into the most intimate place with the Father. There are no layers, no mediators or structures that regulate our relationship with God. It was His own doing to take it out the way, for He desires personal, individual, continual contact with you.

"How did the lessons of history vanish so quickly? When Christianity became the official religion of the Roman Empire, the bishop moved his seat from among the people to the altar. It became the place of honor, power ... and later the throne. Then gradually the clergy even removed worship from the people and kept it for themselves ... while the people watch. Later, the Reformation merely exchanged the priest for a minister and put a sermon in the place of communion. Then, the rest of history simply supported these distortions. The Enlightenment turned preaching into worship, and modern management turned preachers into executives. " Thomas Hohstadt from "Dying to Live – The 21st Century Church."

The temple has ceased to be a physical, geographical centre of worship. Christ is the venue! You are His address! He is the substance that makes our worship tangible.

John 4:23 *"But the time is coming--it has, in fact, come--when what you're called will not matter and where you go to worship will not matter."*

John 2:19-21 *"Jesus answered them, 'Destroy this temple, and in three days I will raise it up.'*

The Jews then said, 'It has taken forty-six years to build this temple, and will you raise it up in three days?' But he was speaking about the temple of his body."

These illustrations just scratch the surface of what Christ's coming accomplished. Let's now examine these in more depth and move into more of the substance of His work. The real value of what He accomplished is not found in external changes, but in what He accomplished in you. He not only changed religious practises, He changed mankind's standing before God! God's audience is not a religious group, but all of humanity ... all of creation.

"This mystery has been kept in the dark for a long time, but now it's out in the open. God wanted everyone, not just Jews, to know this rich and glorious secret inside and out, regardless of their background, regardless of their religious standing. The mystery in a nutshell is just this: Christ is in you " Col 1:26, 27

"God was in Christ, reconciling the world unto himself, not imputing their trespasses unto them" 2 Cor 5:19

Wow! The woooorld is forgiven! When you confess sin, is not when God finds out about it! Neither is your repentance the basis of your forgiveness! The basis is the sacrifice of Christ – that is where God made up His mind about sin: it's dealt with, the slate wiped clean (Col 2:14). *"This is final: I have deleted the record of your sins and misdeeds. I no longer recall them."* (Heb 10:17)

1John 2:2: "*When he served as a sacrifice for our sins, he solved the sin problem for good--not only ours, but the whole world's.*"

1Timothy 4:10: "*For therefore we both labour and suffer reproach, because we trust in the living God, who is the Saviour of all men, specially of those that believe.*"

When a person hears this and responds in faith, then the benefit of it becomes part of his experience. But whether you enjoy the benefit of this truth or not, it is still true!

"*He is kind to the ungrateful and evil*" (Luke 6:35). "*He desires ALL people to be saved*" (1 Timothy 2:4). He "*gave himself as a ransom for ALL*" (1 Timothy 2:6). He "*is not wishing that ANY should perish, but that ALL should reach repentance*" (2 Peter 3:9)

Righteousness came upon all men.

Rom. 5:18: "*Therefore, as by the offence of one, judgement came upon all men to condemnation, even so by the righteousness of one, the free gift came upon all men to justification of life.*"

It will be beneficial to read the whole passage of Rom 5:12–21

The following piece was written in the 1800s so excuse the

use of old English and enjoy the clarity of insight.

"*Paul also says, "For as by one man's disobedience many were made sinners, so by the obedience of one shall many be made righteous." The same many that were made sinners, Paul declares "shall be made righteous." This certainly asserts the justification of all sinners. Parkhurst in his Greek Lexicon, says, Oi polloi, the many, i.e. the multitude, or whole bulk of mankind, Rom. 5:15,19, in which texts oi polloi are plainly equivalent to Pantas anthropous, all men, verses 12, 18." The learned Dr. Macknight is to the same purport. "For as oi polloi, the many, in the first part of the verse, does not mean some of mankind only, but all mankind, from first to last, who without exception, are constituted sinners, so the many in the latter part of the verse, who are said to be constituted righteous, through the obedience of Christ, must mean ALL MANKIND, from the beginning to the end of the world, without exception." See his commentary on the place. The evident sense of the passage is this: For as the many, that is, the whole bulk of mankind were made sinners, so shall the many, that is, the whole bulk of mankind, be made righteous. What can be plainer than this fact? We agree with the authors of the Improved Version, who say, "Nothing can be more obvious than this, that it is the apostle's intention to represent all mankind, without exception, as deriving greater benefit from the mission of Christ, than they suffered injury from the fall of Adam. The universality of the apostle's expression is very remarkable. The same "many" who were made sinners by the disobedience of one, are made righteous by the obedience of*

104

the other. If all men are condemned by the offence of one, the same all are justified by the righteousness of the other. These universal terms, so frequently repeated, and so variously diversified, cannot be reconciled to the limitation of the blessings of the Gospel, to the elect alone, or to a part only of the human race." (Note of Rom. 5:19)"

Jesus has forever changed the state of man before God the Father. The legitimate wall of sin that stood between God and man was removed in Christ. The only separation that remains is man's ignorance and unbelief of this truth. This is our message that has a legitimate claim upon every man. What a confidence that God is making His appeal through us! 2 Cor. 5:20: *"Now then, we serve as ambassadors for Christ, as though God were appealing through us: we implore you on Christ's behalf, be reconciled to God."*

We can do nothing against the truth

There are truths which remain true whether you believe them or not. Paul understood this and wrote *'for we can do nothing against the truth, but only for the truth'* (2 Cor 13:8) In the life, death and resurrection of Jesus, God did something for and with mankind that is immutable – not subject or susceptible to change or variation in form or quality or nature. The success of what He accomplished is unchallenged, unaffected by unbelief. In Christ God removed every obstacle and hindrance that stood between Himself and man. He dealt with sin – all sin of all people. He invalidated guilt – it has no foundation. These are things He did for us, whether we are aware of it or not. But He also did something with us – in His death, we died. In His resurrection we were elevated to a new position of blameless innocence before God. *"There's no end to what has happened in you—it's beyond speech, beyond knowledge."* (1 Cor 1:5 MSG) These things do not become true when you believe them – they are true even if you are unaware of them. Even if no-one believed, the truth about man and God would remain true. *"What if some did not have faith? Will their lack of faith nullify God's faithfulness? Not at all!"* (Rom 3:3)

Fully persuaded

So if the truth remains truth no matter what I believe, does my faith really matter? Absolutely yes, in every way. We only experience the benefit of truth as we embrace it. *"For we also have had the gospel preached to us, just as they did; but the message they heard was of no value to them, because those who heard did not combine it with faith. Now we who have believed enter that rest, just as God has said"* (Heb 4:2) The truth has no value for you individually, if it is not combined with faith. Paul wrote about the 'wealth' or 'riches' of being fully persuaded (Col 2:2) There is a richness of life, a rest of satisfaction, an abundance of contentment, that is only found in being fully persuaded.

Falling in love

Faith is so much more than correct information … as much as falling in love is more than knowing the facts about another person. When I met Mary-Anne, I did not know her date of birth, background nor even how to spell her name! But that did not stop my heart from responding with a 'wow'. When a beautiful landscape appears before me, I instantly respond with appreciation without needing facts and figures. Faith is such a gift – it's an instant response when encountering God. Whenever He reveals Himself, we automatically respond with awe and adoration. Seeing what He sees causes us to believe what He believes. It is so much more than the pathetic 'Statements Of Faith' that some organisations publish. I'm so glad that neither Jesus nor Paul ever wrote a 'Statement of Faith' – they knew that the adoration they had in response to the beauty of the Father could never be reduced to a set of principles or neatly categorised into a doctrine. All we could ever hope to express is an introduction, an invitation for others to see what we see.

For the truth

'for we can do nothing against the truth, but only for the truth' (2 Cor 13:8) Although we can do nothing against the truth, we can do something for it! We can allow it to have its full effect in us and through us. We can draw the maximum value and benefit from it as we combine it with faith, allowing God to persuade us

fully, as He is persuaded. 1Cor 1: 6 speaks about the testimony of Christ that has been confirmed in us.

Why do you think Paul, knowing that we can do nothing against the truth, would still risk his life and endure agonising persecution and torture for the sake of making this truth known. Well, we don't have to guess, he wrote about his motivation. "*For Christ's love compels us, since we have reached this conclusion: if One died for all, then all died. And He died for all so that those who live should no longer live for themselves, but for the One who died for them and was raised.*" (2 Cor 5:14,15) Paul reached a conclusion – the conclusion that, what Christ accomplished, included all mankind … yet the full implication of this truth, the benefit of this truth still eluded the masses because of ignorance. The desire for others to enjoy the full benefit of these immutable truths, drove him to make this truth known as accurately as possible.

So what can we do for the truth? We can allow it to have its full effect in and through us. Allow the testimony of Christ to be confirmed in you. We do this as we continue to live in awe at the revelation brought to us through Jesus Christ. We do this as we allow our enjoyment of Him to overflow into loving others – a love that compels us to live for more than just ourselves.

The full value and benefit of the truth will be realised. He is not pressed by time or impatient to draw all men to Himself

– He has all eternity to show us the full value and benefit of what He accomplished on our behalf *"so that in the coming ages He might display the immeasurable riches of His grace in His kindness to us in Christ Jesus."* until *"all created beings in heaven and on earth—even those long ago dead and buried—will bow in worship before this Jesus Christ, and call out in praise that he is the Master of all, to the glorious honor of God the Father"* (Eph 2:7; Phil 2:10,11)

Christ - The Source

The most accurate translation happened when the eternal Word of God was translated into flesh – a living text. The mystery has been revealed: God never intended to live in books or institutions, but to write His thoughts upon our hearts – Christ in you!

"Bottled at Source' is the proud statement printed on the bottle of spring water I hold in my hand. The rest of the message emphasises how this water contains no additives or contaminants, but only the natural goodness found at the source – the unpolluted origin. The message is clear: the further from the source, the greater the potential for contamination; the closer to the source, the purer.

This is the same idea Paul had about the message he preached. *"Now I want you to know, brothers, that the gospel preached by me is not based on a human point of view. For I did not receive it from a human source and I was not taught it, but it came by a revelation of Jesus Christ."* Galatians 1:11,12

The first chapter of this letter and much of the second is focused on this concept that no human taught him this message, neither was it the product of his own scholastic efforts. Rather, this message was initiated and communicated by God directly – he received it from the source … unpolluted, original, authoritative, pure. This gospel is not subject to human interpretation, translation or misrepresentation.

He goes through great lengths to explain that he had no prolonged contact with any of the recognised leaders – in summary: *"But from those recognised as important (what they really were makes no difference to me; God does not show favoritism)—those recognised as important added nothing to*

112
me." (2:6)

Paul obviously understood the importance of direct, unrestricted contact with the Light of life as apposed to a second-hand religious system that attempts to communicate truth through a man-made hierarchy. Now he undoubtedly thought it important to communicate this message, but the whole purpose of his communication (and mine) was to introduce the listeners to the Source of these truths and not to set himself up as the source of their spiritual understanding. His attitude is portrayed so clearly in this portion of one of his letters: *"We're not in charge of how you live out the faith, looking over your shoulders, suspiciously critical. We're partners, working alongside you, joyfully expectant. I know that you stand by your own faith, not by ours."* 2 Cor 1:24 MSG

This seems to me a very different approach to that taken by many religious institutions. Most of these institutions regard themselves, consciously or unconsciously, as the guardians of truth – desiring to control and mediate between their followers and God. In the process these religious systems have become contaminants of the original message – no longer containing the pure message as derived from the source, but mixed with the additives of human tradition and popular interpretation.

No father desires a relationship with his children to be interfered with through a third party broker – speaking to his children via an interpreter. The Father, your Creator, desires a direct open relationship with you personally. He is confident in the ability He gave you to hear Him and respond .

Jesus, seeing the emptiness of religious festivals and rituals offered a much better alternative. "*On the last and most important day of the festival, Jesus stood up and cried out, "If anyone is thirsty, he should come to Me and drink! The one who believes in Me, as the Scripture has said, will have streams of living water flow from deep within him.*" John 7:37,38

The original, accurate translation

The most accurate translation happened when the eternal Word of God was translated into flesh – a living text. The mystery has been revealed: God never intended to live in books or institutions, but to write His thoughts upon our hearts – Christ in you!

What translation did Peter, Paul or John use? The text that captivated their minds and hearts was the living text – the word made flesh. To read Him, to interpret Him, to understand Him and to explain Him was no academic exercise, but rather a living and real relationship.

The scriptures bear witness to this living text; the scriptures point to a reality greater than themselves, a translation more accurate than words can ever convey.

Discover Christ in you and read Him, meditate upon Him, understand Him and explain Him. And feel free to use whatever textual translation you want to, as long as you read it in the context of Christ in you – the implanted Word; the 100% accurate translation.

Ekklesia and Christ

God doesn't want to just live in you!.....He wants to live through you. You were designed not only to contain Him, but to express Him. God is light and light shines - don't limit Him to a hidden inner life, allow Him to shine through your everyday conversations; to think His thoughts through you; to be Himself through yourself.

A flower blooming in your garden is a unique expression of many different ingredients such as the sun, water, and earth. Although it is a beautiful expression of these qualities, the whole ecosystem that made this flower possible is infinitely greater than just this flower. The flower will soon fade and die, but creation continues.

When we speak about church, we have to look far beyond the local assembly (that many refer to as church), limited to time and space, before we can truly understand this. The local assembly is spoken of in scripture, but much more is said about the infinitely greater realities of which the local assembly is simply an expression.

We will, therefore, first look at the realities regarding ekklesia (church), beyond its temporal expression in a local assembly. Once these truths are grasped our expression of them will be much more accurate and beautiful. Trying to emulate the local assemblies we see in the N.T. without appreciating the realities that birthed these assemblies will leave us with lifeless, meaningless, yet biblically correct assemblies! By this I mean the form will be there, but not the life. The appearance might be correct, but the fruit will be missing as per the fig tree that Jesus cursed.

'Ekklesia' is the Greek word most often translated as 'church' in the New Testament. In plain usage it meant an assembly.

Interestingly it is made up of two root words, the first being:

ek, ex

A primary preposition denoting origin (the point whence motion or action proceeds), from, out

And the second part being:

kal-eh'-o

to "call" (properly aloud, but used in a variety of applications, directly or otherwise): - bid, call (forth), (whose, whose sur-) name (was [called]).

It implies being named by our origin. From our origin proceeds a call; from our Creator comes a claim upon our existence. Our Father names us and what He calls us is more valid than any other name or identity we might have adopted. Eph. 3:15 reveals that all families, races and nations of man are named by the Father. The same words are used namely 'ek' (from whom) and the word 'named'.

Eph 3:15: "*Of whom the whole family in heaven and earth is named*"

Firstly, we have to say, based on this and many other scriptures, that the Father's call is for every person; His claim is upon all mankind for He knows their true identity; He is the origin from whom this call proceeds. It then follows that those who respond to His call, those who acknowledge their true identity in Him, become the manifested form of this ekklesia.

Jesus had a few things to say about ekklesia:

Mat 16:13-18: "*When Jesus arrived in the villages of Caesarea Philippi, he asked his disciples, "What are people saying about who the Son of Man is?"*

They replied, "Some think he is John the Baptizer, some say Elijah, some Jeremiah or one of the other prophets."

He pressed them, "And how about you? Who do you say I am?"

Simon Peter said, "You're the Christ, the Messiah, the Son of the living God."

Jesus came back, "God bless you, Simon, son of Jonah! You didn't get that answer out of books or from teachers. My Father in heaven, God himself, let you in on this secret of who I really am. And now I'm going to tell you who you are, really are. You are Peter, a rock. This is the rock on which I will put together my church, a church so expansive with energy that not even the gates of hell will be able to keep it out.""

Can you see how the true identity of Jesus, and the true identity of man is the revelation upon which Jesus builds His church. The Father revealed to Simon that the Son of Man is indeed the Son of God. He, however, only saw its significance in relation to Jesus. Jesus does not leave this here, but takes the revelation a step further. This is not only a revelation regarding the identity of Jesus, but also a revelation regarding the identity of man.

Jesus speaks very specifically to Peter regarding his identity. He starts by referring to him as "*Simon, son of Jonah*" With this Jesus confirms that he too is a son of man – it was not a special title reserved for Jesus. But then he draws him into a deeper understanding of his identity. "*You are Peter*" 'Peter' meaning a piece of a rock. Jesus uses a different word the second time He refers to rock. He does not use the word 'piece of rock' but refers to the actual big rock from which the piece came. Isaiah 51:1: "*Listen to me, all you who are serious about right living and committed to seeking GOD. Ponder the rock from which you were cut, the quarry from which you were dug.*" "*...respond to the greatness of our God! The Rock: His works are perfect.*"

Deut 32:3,4

Jesus challenges Peter to consider his own origin beyond his natural birth and come to the same conclusion concerning himself as the conclusion he came to concerning Christ, namely: the son of man (son of Jonah in this case) is also the son of God!

"*Upon this rock*" – the rock from which you were cut – your origin, I will build my church and not even the gates of hell (hades) will be able to stand against this. Whatever literal place is meant with the word Hades, there is also a very significant meaning beyond this. The word 'hades' is made of two words that mean 'to see' and the negative form of it. So figuratively it means 'not to see' or ignorance! Thus, ignorance will not be able to stand before the revelation of your true identity.

John 1:4,5: "*In Him was life; and the life was the light of men. And the light shineth in darkness; and the darkness comprehended it not.*"

Jesus came and lived life as an open display of who and what man originally was intended to be. This open manifestation of life as it was intended, appeals to every man's conscience, because there remains in man a divine spark despite the fall. This same appeal is extended through those who responded to this call, and so Paul writes concerning his life "*but by manifestation of the truth commending ourselves to every man's conscience in the sight of God*" (2Cor 4:2).

When Paul writes about this ekklesia in the letter to the Ephesians, he uses the picture of a body of which Christ is the Head. What he describes is not just a local assembly. He does not start with the form or the method through which these truths are expressed, but rather with the bigger picture of what it is really about.

God desires to express Himself! God wants a body! Your body is not some remote controlled object apart from your head. You are one. In this same way the Father planned, and took pleasure in this plan, and He chose man as the ideal container for Himself ... but more than a container. God doesn't want to just live in you ... He wants to live through you! You were designed not only to contain Him, but to express Him. God is light and light shines - don't limit Him to a hidden, inner life, allow Him to shine through your everyday conversations; to think His thoughts through you; to be Himself through yourself. Eph 1: 18 reveals that God has an inheritance and that inheritance is in man! He designed us as the ultimate expression of Himself. How large, varied, deep, wide, broad and long is God's expression of Himself? Can you measure Him? This must bring us to the conclusion that we should never seek to control, limit or define how God is to express Himself through the church, lest we make it an expression of ourselves, rather than an expression of Him. The head, Christ, alone directs and inspires each individual part to do whatever He desires. How often have we tried to displace Christ with methods of our own making.

Ekklesia is so much more than the final expression of it in a local body. We will look at the local body later, but first let us see deeper into what ekklesia really is.

1Cor. 12:12: "*Even as the body is one, and has many members, but all the members of the one body, being many, are one body, so also is Christ.*"

Christ is no longer an individual! Read 1 Cor. 12:12 again and again until you see it. Christ now consists of many members, making one body. You are a part of what makes Christ, Christ.

It is for this reason that we should never dishonour Christ by equating Him with an organisation. Only 'that' which is made in His likeness and image has the ablity of expressing His likeness and image. When we speak of church we speak of Christ, or at least a part of Christ, and Christ is not an event or a program or an organisation made by human hands. He is a person in whom the fullness of the godhead dwells in bodily form.

Ekklesia from God's point of view is not a temporary arrangement. Eph 3:19-21 reveals that God purposes to manifest Himself through us in ways we have not imagined and that this demonstration of who He is, will continue throughout all ages to come.

Eph 3:19-21 *"And to know the love of Christ, which passeth knowledge, that ye might be filled with all the fullness of God. Now unto him that is able to do exceeding abundantly above all that we ask or think, according to the power that worketh in us, unto him be glory in the church by Christ Jesus throughout all ages, world without end."*

Church, as a local body, is a temporal manifestation of real church, which is eternal. Heb 12:23 shows that ekklesia includes the assembly of the spirits of just men. So church as God knows it, is not limited to the here and now of this temporal realm. His church is eternal.

A Fresh Expression of Ekklesia

"We're not in charge of how you live out the faith, looking over your shoulders, suspiciously critical. We're partners, working alongside you, joyfully expectant. I know that you stand by your own faith, not by ours."

2 Cor 1:24 MSG

Our expression of ekklesia (church) is really an expression of Christ. People throughout the ages, and at this present time throughout the world, have discovered that this expression can never be reduced to a human formula; to a man-made structure or program.

An authentic encounter with Christ will lead to an authentic expression of Christ. So, are there any guidelines or patterns that can be followed? Most of these questions totally miss the point. How we 'do church' is not relevant at all until we clearly appreciate who we are expressing. Once our focus is clearly and consistently on Him, then we can rest assured that our expression of Him, no matter how different, will be true. So now we can ask this question again. What should an expression of ekklesia look like?

It is a question which is more easily answered by saying what it should not look like. The creativity of God; the wealth of Christ is far too large to limit to a set procedure or a specific form. We do know this: the message of Christ will not be contradicted by a true expression of Christ.

A fresh appreciation of our equality.

One of the most peculiar and radical characteristics of this message was (and is) the way in which all men were equally valued. Imagine those first gatherings in homes where the slave sat next to his master, and the gentile next to a Jew in equal position before the Father! Where you came from, what you earned – all these human measures were irrelevant in the light of a new definition of man's worth. Christ now defines us!

The very heart of the message of Christ is the equality and brotherhood of all mankind. Christianity was the first 'religion' that had no professional priesthood. The very hierarchies that separated mankind from direct contact with the Father were removed by the Father Himself, and this was confirmed when He tore the curtain of separation in the temple.

Seeing that this is at the very heart of Christ's message, any system that once again builds hierarchies of authority and levels of importance, is without a doubt not an expression of Christ, but a man-made counterfeit. If we have not learned how to be brothers of equal standing, we will continue to be trapped in an environment of comparison that gives birth to either pride or inferiority. Both pride and inferiority come from not appreciating God's opinion of you, but rather comparing yourself to others. "*For we are not bold to number or compare ourselves with certain of them that commend themselves: but they themselves, measuring themselves by themselves, and comparing themselves with themselves, are without understanding.*" (2 Cor 10 : 12)

Once this truth is clearly appreciated, then we can appreciate the diversity and uniqueness of one-another's gifts and functions. We now see in each other unique expressions of the gifts and character of Christ, of whose fullness we have received and we are complete in Him. No room remains for competition.

A new appreciation of our freedom.

In Paul's letter to the Romans he addressed some very real issues that developed in that community of believers. Let's first get a more accurate picture of what a meeting looked like at that time (chances are that many have a very different idea of 'meeting' than what happened here). Most of these meetings included a meal – a real meal with a symbolic meaning, not a symbolic meal with a 'real' meaning. The diversity of people, suddenly becoming so close to one-another, gave much opportunity for friction. How people ate, what they ate and drank differed greatly, and some felt it their duty to teach the underprivileged some manners.

Paul addresses this situation with such an insightful appreciation of the freedom we have discovered in Christ. His confidence in Christ's ability to transform lives without our interference is simply refreshing. Herewith his letter:

"Welcome with open arms fellow believers who don't see things the way you do. And don't jump all over them every time they do or say something you don't agree with--even when it seems that

they are strong on opinions but weak in the faith department. Remember, they have their own history to deal with. Treat them gently. For instance, a person who has been around for a while might well be convinced that he can eat anything on the table, while another, with a different background, might assume all Christians should be vegetarians and eat accordingly. But since both are guests at Christ's table, wouldn't it be terribly rude if they fell to criticizing what the other ate or didn't eat? God, after all, invited them both to the table.

Do you have any business crossing people off the guest list or interfering with God's welcome? If there are corrections to be made or manners to be learned, God can handle that without your help. Or, say, one person thinks that some days should be set aside as holy and another thinks that each day is pretty much like any other. There are good reasons either way. So, each person is free to follow the convictions of conscience.

What's important in all this is that if you keep a holy day, keep it for God's sake; if you eat meat, eat it to the glory of God and thank God for prime rib; if you're a vegetarian, eat vegetables to the glory of God and thank God for broccoli. None of us are permitted to insist on our own way in these matters.

It's God we are answerable to--all the way from life to death and everything in between--not each other.

That's why Jesus lived and died and then lived again: so that he could be our Master across the entire range of life and death, and free us from the petty tyrannies of each other.

So where does that leave you when you criticise a brother? And where does that leave you when you condescend to a sister? I'd say it leaves you looking pretty silly--or worse. Eventually, we're all going to end up kneeling side by side in the place of judgment, facing God. Your critical and condescending ways aren't going to improve your position there one bit. Read it for yourself in Scripture: "As I live and breathe," God says, "every knee will bow before me; Every tongue will tell the honest truth that I and only I am God."

So tend to your knitting. You've got your hands full just taking care of your own life before God. Forget about deciding what's right for each other. Here's what you need to be concerned about: that you don't get in the way of someone else, making life more difficult than it already is.

I'm convinced--Jesus convinced me!--that everything as it is in itself is holy. We, of course, by the way we treat it or talk about it, can contaminate it. If you confuse others by making a big issue over what they eat or don't eat, you're no longer a companion with them in love, are you? These, remember, are persons for whom Christ died. Would you risk sending them to hell over an item in their diet? Don't you dare let a piece of God-blessed food become an occasion of soul-poisoning!

> God's kingdom isn't a matter of what you put in your stomach, for goodness' sake. It's what God does with your life as he sets it right, puts it together, and completes it with joy."

Rom 14:1-17

There are a few statements that emphasises this attitude and are worth repeating:

> "Welcome with open arms fellow believers who don't see things the way you do. And don't jump all over them every time they do or say something you don't agree with ... If there are corrections to be made or manners to be learned, God can handle that without your help ... So, each person is free to follow the convictions of conscience ... None of us are permitted to insist on our own way in these matters. It's God we are answerable to--all the way from life to death and everything in between--not each other. That's why Jesus lived and died and then lived again: so that he could be our Master across the entire range of life and death, and free us from the petty tyrannies of each other ...So tend to your knitting. You've got your hands full just taking care of your own life before God. Forget about deciding what's right for each other."

What an attitude! May we grow up into this same attitude. Some might think that such an attitude is only appropriate for some, but we still need some leaders that have the right to interfere at will. Well, I would consider Paul an authority in this regard, and if his attitude was such that he respected the individual's freedom, I see no reason to justify any other attitude.

There is good reason for him having such an attitude. If we could grasp the reason behind this attitude it will help us greatly. In another letter he gives us this insight: "*We're not in charge of how you live out the faith, looking over your shoulders, suspiciously critical. We're partners, working alongside you, joyfully expectant. I know that you stand by your own faith, not by ours.*" 2 Cor 1:24

We live in the joyful expectation that God is at work in others. We believe the best of one another because of this persuasion. Our communication is based around the acknowledgement of every good thing that is in us, in Christ. "*that the sharing of your faith may be based upon and promote full recognition and appreciation and understanding and precise knowledge of every good thing that is ours in Christ Jesus*" (Philemon 1:6)

Obviously Father can instruct us to speak and correct in love occasionally, but as Paul we should do this 'with much tears'. If your eyes are dry, you should consider carefully if this is Father inspiring you. Don't confuse a critical attitude with God-inspired compassion – the difference could not be greater.

A fresh understanding of authority.

Once we understand our common standing before Father and appreciate each other in this environment of equality; once we have grown into this attitude of respecting each other's personal freedom and live in the joyful expectation of Father working in us; once we are grounded and established in these truths, then and only then will we see authority in its true context.

Our understanding of authority will either be a liberating, releasing and empowering insight or a bondage that limits our expression and keeps us enslaved to the opinions of others. The probability that all of us have seen some perverted form of authority is great. Authority is one of the most abused subjects in the Word, and that's why we need to see it from God's perspective.

It is the love of a father that motivates him to share more and more of his resources with his children. As a father longs for his children to be empowered to act and speak with integrity, so our heavenly Father desires to share His powers with us. No parent wants to nurture a child in such a way that the child never learns to think and act on his or her own. Parents want their children to mature in such a way that resources and power can be entrusted to them. Love is therefore the motivating force out of which authority develops.

The God-kind of authority is the means by which God enables, releases and empowers us to become all He knows us to be. His authority is not used to control, but to entrust; His authority does not limit our expression, but draws out the most creative abilities in us. His authority does not even look like most authority we have seen before; it simply looks like love in action.

Those who enjoy friendship with Father do not fear His authority, because it is just another expression of His love. To trust His authority is easy, for we know and believe the love He has for us. The difficulty for most is how to relate to authority in other people. How does He communicate His authority through other people. The reason for this becomes clear as we discover in God's Word the two ways in which authority is communicated.

Most only know of one type of authority and that is the hierarchical type, where authority is delegated from one level to another. But there is another type! The difference is as broad and definite as the difference between the old and the new covenant.

Lets first hear what Jesus had to say about this:

Mat 20:25 - 28 *"But Jesus called them unto him, and said, Ye know that the princes of the Gentiles exercise dominion over them, and they that are great exercise authority upon them. But it shall not be so among you: but whosoever will be great among you, let him be your minister; And whosoever will be chief among you, let him be your servant: Even as the Son of man came not to be ministered unto, but to minister, and to give his life a ransom for many."*

Here Jesus introduces us to the first way in which authority is manifested. Let's call it the organisational or hierarchical type. He describes it as authority 'over' or dominion 'over' indicating that it is bound to a position, which in turn is bound to a level. Now the most significant words in this passage that we cannot miss is: *'... it shall not be so among you ...'* Did you get that? IT SHALL NOT BE SO AMONG YOU.

Jesus introduced a whole new way in which His authority operates among us. Whereas the organisational type of authority was bound to a position and therefore whoever filled the position had the authority, independent of his character, this new type is linked to a function or task. Let's call it organic or fluid authority for now.

To illustrate this, I'll use Paul's metaphor for the church, which is a body. If you decide to move your fingers, you don't first communicate the thought to your arm, which in turn communicates it to your hand, which in turn communicates it to your fingers. That's ridiculous. Every part of your body is directly linked to the head and is well able to receive instructions directly. There are no 'positions' of greater authority through which these instructions need to be filtered to find out if they really came from the head. There is only one authority, and that is the head. He empowers certain parts of the body to do certain tasks. That authority does not continue to reside in that part of the body, neither does it elevate that part over other parts. The parts of the body are equal among one another.

"*But it's obvious by now, isn't it, that Christ's church is a complete Body and not a gigantic, unidimensional Part? It's not all Apostle, not all Prophet, not all Miracle Worker, not all Healer, not all Prayer in Tongues, not all Interpreter of Tongues. And yet some of you keep competing for so-called "important" parts. But now I want to lay out a far better way for you.*" 1 Corinthians 12:29-31

Official versus relational.

In the organisational system, authority is delegated to a position without much regard to the changing character of the person filling the position. Whoever fills the position stands within the authority of that position for as long as he retains the position. This is the type of authority we see in the Old Testament, religious hierarchies and within the current governmental institutions. A dramatic example of how a person can personally violate God's commands, and still retain authority is that of Saul. Even after the Word tells us that the spirit of God departed from him, he still retained the authority of his position, and therefore, David still showed respect because of the position he was in.

This is one of the major problems with that system, therefore, God changed it in the way His 'ekklesia', church operates. The organisational model is dependant on titles and official positions without much connection to the current spiritual condition of the person filling the post.

In all of Paul's letters to the churches, he seems completely unaware of any organisational structures. There were many words available to Paul that could express position and official leadership, but he deliberately chose not to use one of them. Here are some examples:

The word 'arche' which means a ruler or leader, specifically related to rank, is completely absent from all his writings. The greek word 'time' means officer or dignitary – nowhere to be found. 'telos' the inherent power or authority of a ruler (authority related to position) – he never describes any believer in this way. 'archisunagogus' is a synagogue official or religious official. Surely this would have been a useful way to describe church leadership? Sorry, but the New Testament is absolutely quiet. 'hazzan' means a public worship leader. Just about every organised church I have visited, have one of these. Surely it must be in the Bible!

My apologies, Paul was obviously not as sophisticated as we are! 'taxis' means a post, position or rank. Now, although we have found these words very useful to bring order in congregations, we have one small problem: they are not in the New Testament! 'hierateia' means a priest's office. Once again, completely missing from the New Testament, when describing the church.

Could it be possible that they took the words of Jesus seriously when He said that organisational type authority would not be the way His church operates?

Mat 20:25 - 28 *"But Jesus called them unto him, and said, Ye know that the princes of the Gentiles exercise dominion over them, and they that are great exercise authority upon them. But it shall not be so among you: but whosoever will be great among you, let him be your minister; And whosoever will be chief among you, let him be your servant: Even as the Son of man came not to be ministered unto, but to minister, and to give his life a ransom for many."*

The most popular word used by the apostles to describe church 'leaders' is 'diakonos' which means servant!

Organic authority is rich in words that describe function. Words like serving, shepherding and overseeing. The God kind of authority is recognised in what it does. Organic authority knows nothing about title or position. Just as your hand does not require a new title or official position to obey the head, so our relation to Christ has no connection to official positions. The idea that there are professional positions of authority in the body of Christ, and the rest are just 'laymen' is contrary to the scriptures. In 1 Peter 2:9, Peter declares every believer to be part of a royal priesthood. We all have exactly the same access to the Father!

To conclude: Organic authority is linked to function. It is fluid because it is much more linked to the character of the person, specifically his serving and childlike meekness. Position and titles are completely missing from this concept.

Organisational authority is rigid and based on a top-down level, without much connection to the attitude or character of the person filling the position.

Responsibility versus mindless obedience.

Positional authority takes away much of the responsibility of those in subjection to it. Official authority does not have much space for discussion. It is only concerned with a simple response of 'Yes' or 'No'. The subordinate is discouraged from asking if instructions are right or wrong; the responsibility of whether they are right or wrong lies with the official that gave the instructions. This system keeps its subjects in continual immaturity. No wonder Jesus changed this system in the church.

He believes in every person's ability to personally hear, and respond to His voice.

It is actually much easier to just walk in the slip-stream of another person's relationship with God. It requires much less effort to thoughtlessly obey than to take responsibility yourself for what you believe and do.

Do you realise that Paul's letters to the churches were never addressed to the leaders of the church! They were addressed to the whole church without any official acknowledgement of local leaders. It's as if He did not know of their existence! The reason is: they did not exist in the way we have re-introduced them! Even when He addressed serious problems, he addressed the whole group of believers, the whole church, and encouraged them to solve it. He never removed the responsibility from the individual person, and placed it on a select few.

Can you imagine what would happen in most of our modern day 'churches' if someone wrote a letter to be read to the whole church without first informing the officials of its content! In this letter, he addresses the issues that everyone is avoiding and he makes no mention of leaders! Paul would have been labelled a heretic by most of our organisations.

I mean, does he not know that baby Christians can't deal with these real issues! And how dare he speak to my people without my permission. These things should be dealt with secretly by the select few who can decide on behalf of everyone else.

Well, obviously these New Testament churches did not exist in the form many exist in today. Paul spoke to them as equals and encouraged them all to take responsibility for one another. His confidence in ALL is reflected throughout his writings:

2 Corinthians 7:16: "*I rejoice that in all things I have confidence in you all.*"

Rom 15:14: "*And I myself also am persuaded of you, my brethren, that ye also are full of goodness, filled with all knowledge, able also to admonish one another.*"

Conclusion: Organisational authority removes much responsibility from its subjects and therefore keeps them immature.

Organic authority believes in the ability of each part of the body to hear instructions from the head. Everyone is therefore placed in an environment of personal responsibility and, therefore, growth.

Subordination versus voluntary submission

Paul never pulled rank in his communication to believers.

In fact his attitude towards organisational authority becomes strikingly clear in the book of Galatians. In chapter 1 and 2 Paul describes how this message was not delivered, or explained to him by any other man, but by revelation. (there was no hierarchy of revelation) To those who thought the apostolic ministry (servanthood, lest we forget) is just another way to justify positions and titles in the church, Paul leaves us with a sobering comment.

Gal. 2:6: *"As for those (the other apostles) who were considered important in the church, their reputation doesn't concern me. God isn't impressed with mere appearances, and neither am I. And of course these leaders were able to add nothing to the message I had been preaching."*

Those who cannot see beyond hierarchical type of authority might think that Paul could say this, because He was uniquely chosen and placed on an equal or higher level than the other apostles. But let's read his words again "God isn't impressed with mere appearances, and neither am I". It has nothing to do with position or title, because that is man-made. God does not regard it, and therefore we should not regard it either!

Organic authority uses the language of persuasion; it has no title to rest on, so its appeal is to the conscience of man.

2 Cor. 8:8: *"I'm not trying to order you around against your*

will. But by bringing in the Macedonians' enthusiasm as a stimulus to your love, I am hoping to bring the best out of you."

Philemon 1:8,9 *"For this reason I could be bold enough, as your brother in Christ, to order you to do what should be done. But because I love you, I make a request instead."*

Rom. 12:1 *"So then, my friends, because of God's great mercy to us I appeal to you..."*

Rom. 15:30 *"I urge you, friends ..."*

1 Cor. 1:10 *"By the authority of our Lord Jesus Christ I appeal to all of you, my friends"*

This is not the language of a superior religious official, ordering the ignorant masses how and what to believe. This is the language of a friend, an equal, appealing and urging his brothers to be persuaded by the truth.

Conclusion: To voluntarily submit to the appeal of a friend is the way in which God wants His authority to be manifested among us. Eph. 5:21: *"And be submissive one to another, in the love of the Messiah."* We voluntarily recognise and respect the authority of God in one another. It is a beautiful thing to see.

Organisational authority legitimately exists in the world and we are told to obey our governments in the scriptures, but in the church such authority is a perversion of what God desires. This does not mean He does not bless people involved in those organisations, it simply means they miss out on His best. When Israel rejected God's personal rule over them, and chose a King instead, He still blessed them as much as He could. They did, however, endure a lot of hardship because they rejected His theocratic (organic) type of rule and chose instead the organisational type.

Go for God's best! Live in the constant awareness of zero distance between you and Him. Respect and value all men alike; their outward appearance means nothing to God and neither to us!

It is also possible that organisations exist (I know of some) for the exclusive purpose of promoting this gospel. Such organisations do not pretend to be church - they exist to serve the *church*, which is much greater than any organisation.

Focus.

There are certain values that I have come to greatly appreciate in the small-group type gatherings. The simplicity of such groups, is an ideal environment for our focus to remain on the message. It is the message that excites and enthuses us, not the fact that we are doing something new or different. To appreciate Christ in one-another, to stir up faith, and demonstrate love are the reasons for us getting together. It is so easy to fall into the routine of just being together, without making a demand upon yourself to draw out the best out of your brothers and sisters around you. Obviously, this is as much of a danger in small groups as in big groups, however, the simplicity of small groups makes it much easier to remain focused on why we get together.

Spontaneity.

There has been such emphasis placed on finding, or adopting a vision, and then doing whatever it takes to serve that vision faithfully. Pursuing purpose has become, for many, more important than knowing Christ. There is a beautiful balance found in the Scriptures between long term vision and immediate guidance. "Your Word is a lamp to my feet, and a light to my path" Psalms. 119:105. Yes, the Lord wants you to have some light to your path, some insight into the direction He is leading you into, but never at the expense of the immediate relationship with Him. If a person is more excited about a vision, than about the indwelling Christ, something is wrong! The light He gives to our path, is just enough for us to still be dependent upon the lamp to our feet. We undoubtedly still need to hear him daily to walk in the path He has prepared.

This is another value, which is much more naturally cultivated in a small group. Big groups need big visions to excite people, yet they should be broad enough to include as many as possible. Encouraging individuals to hear God for their daily lives becomes very dangerous to the organisation's vision. Forgetting about Christ, and relationship with one another, becomes very likely in a situation where a vision is pursued. I find the ability of a small group to play-it-by-ear very refreshing – it is simply the best environment for spontaneity to thrive in. Every meeting is therefore unique, and being able to listen and change direction is not only exciting for the group, but must be very refreshing for the Father also (I don't think He has much of a say in many of the meetings where the program is set beforehand).

Relationship.

Exchanging pleasantries before an hour's lecture and chatting for 5 minutes afterwards, does not qualify as 'fellowship'. Real, authentic relationship is another treasure that is much more likely to be found in the small group setting. The close proximity and the natural setting of a house means that there is very little room for being fake. In the group I regularly meet with, we also make sure that no one feels obliged to come. There are no sarcastic comments when someone misses a meeting or two. People come because they want to, without a sense of obligation or guilt. The fact that we often share a meal together removes any feeling of a formal meeting. Many of us meet during other times in the week, simply because we are friends! I had very little time for such meetings, or even for my family while involved as a leader in a organisation that believed your commitment to it, is more important than any other relationship. Obviously, this is never said, but if you find yourself without time for your family and friends because of involvement with a 'church organisation', something is wrong.

This message, the message of our Father's favour over us, His children, this message of how He came to indwell us, and lift us to His own level, has everything within it to produce a meaningful life of love. We don't have to artificially try to govern and control what God Himself will do in and through the lives of those who have received Him. Our responsibility is to awaken this life in one another, to acknowledge Christ in one another and trust the working of the Father to do, in one another, what we can't.

Now

"...Now faith is ..."

Heb 11:1

Forget about trying to find His plan for your life – your life is His plan! Neither you location nor your timing matters – He has dawned His eternal day. You are His moment; you are His location! "*...worship the Father neither here at this mountain nor there ... It's who you are...*" John 4:21-23 MSG

Our hope is no longer connected to a future date but to a person within us – all that we could ever have hoped for! Christ in you the hope of glory!

There is nothing in your future that can add anything to you! "*...the world, life, death, the present, the future—all of it is yours...*" 1 Cor 3:22 MSG. Therefore you can remove the focus of every expectation you ever had based on a future date, and instead place it on the One who is within you. The greatest gift the future holds is the unveiling of the reality within you – Christ!

Eternity entered time when God became man. The event of Christ is described as the fullness of time in Eph 1. This means that time can no longer add to the completeness of what He already accomplished for us!

The only value remaining in the past or the future, is its ability to connect you with the present ... I AM. The time-context in which God desires to encounter with you is made plain in His name: I AM! He desires for you to become conscious of this same moment – I AM. Not 'I will be'; Not 'I used to be'; Not 'I hope to be' But the overwhelming awareness that I AM. I am all He ever purposed for me to be. I have all He ever purposed for me to have.

"Today this Scripture is fulfilled in your hearing." (Luke 4:21) The fulfillment of scripture has nothing to do with a calendar anymore – it has everything to do with your hearing!

Discover that the eternal One made His home in you, giving you access to eternity in this moment. Eternity has nothing to do with endless time – it has everything to do with the quality of fellowship and unity with God. (John 17:3)

He who grasps (understands) the Son, grasps eternal life. He who does not grasp the Son, does not grasp life. (1 John 5:12)

More resources available at:

www.hearhim.net

To **download Music & Lyrics** go to:

http://hearhim.net/wordpress/music/

To **download books & literature** go to:

http://hearhim.net/wordpress/book-downloads/

To **subsribe to email notifications**, go to:

http://www.hearhim.net/mail/?p=subscribe

For online conversations and study material see:

schoolofgrace.net

Lightning Source UK Ltd.
Milton Keynes UK
UKOW041137090712

195685UK00006B/11/P